Bethany Joyce Temple

BETHANY
"TEMPLE OF GOD"

BETHANY
"TEMPLE OF GOD"

Copyright © 2023 Bethany Joyce Temple

ISBN 978-1-946683-57-1
Library of Congress Control Number 2023915415

Rapier Publishing Company
Dothan, Alabama 36301

www.rapierpublishing.com
Facebook: www.rapierpublishing@gmail.com
Twitter: rapierpublishing@rapierpub

Printed in the United States of America
All rights reserved under the International Copyright Law. Contents and/or cover may not be reproduced in whole or in part in any form without the consent of the Publisher or Author.

Book Cover Design: Daniel Ojedokun
Book Layout: Rapture Graphics

DEDICATION

I dedicate my book BETHANY "TEMPLE OF GOD," to my five children and their families. I want them to know my heart and my love for them. My heart has always been centered on my children through everything we went through. Like any mother, I want the best for each one of them. When they lack certain things, my heart aches in these areas. The disappointments and misunderstandings in their little minds and hearts are like stabs to my heart. Tears are in my eyes as I write this. I was looking through this 2023-year calendar, and tears of love flowed from my eyes as I came across each child's birthday. I saw the ages of each child. It seems like their ages should be my age.

-Time does not stand still! Where did the time go?-

How much of their lives I missed! My heart is full. How much more are their hearts broken? Life growing up is natural. My heart is blessed to see and know how my children have stayed together, living close to each other. It is the love of God in their hearts. I would like to think that I am partly the reason for raising them in the house of God. It is my life I have lived before them.

Thank God for the memories I have of my children. I can picture each one in my mind, my thoughts from their births to Dion's graduation. The boys, Sidney and Tony, were in high school. Amy was twelve when Shanara was born in 1987. I love my children from the beginning throughout eternity, always.

-Bethany Joyce Temple-

IN MEMORY

In memory of all the men, women, boys, and girls who have gone through some type heartbreak for whatever reason.

We cannot take back time. We can enjoy memories of good times and not dwell on the past. Let us treasure every precious moment for our time that remains in our life. Let us forgive and forget. The Holy Spirit heals; He is our comforter. He mends our broken hearts as if they were never broken. We need to savor the time that we have. We will soon be together in the Kingdom of God, never to separate again.

I want to acknowledge my nephew, William Byron Temple, who we call BB. I mention him in my first book, "G.I. Temple: Soldier of Faith and the Pearl." Byron passed away in August 2022. He was an honor student throughout his years of education. He was a parish librarian in St. Joseph, Louisiana. Byron, BB, received the Holy Ghost under the Elm tree in our front yard, as referenced in my book, "G.I. Temple: Soldier of Faith and the Pearl."

ACKNOWLEDGMENTS

I appreciate my special friend who I was introduced to him at our July 2021 Temple Family Reunion. He has been my special friend from then to this day, 2023.

He is not a preacher; he is a "man of God." He had talked to God that he wanted a Christian wife. The enemy has fought God's will for his life. He has stayed faithful to God, wanting a Christian wife for retirement. We give all glory and praise to God for the great things He has done for us.

A special thanks to God our Father, His Son, Jesus Christ our soon coming King, and the Holy Spirit. We will rise together to meet our Lord in the air. Oh, what a great homecoming day!

I give special thanks to God for our last five Temple siblings. These are the last five: Margaret Willaminta Temple, James DeVonne Temple, Sr., Linda Gail Diane Temple Bueltel, Boyce Dale Temple, Sr., and Bethany Joyce Temple.

Thanks to my sister, Minta Temple, for the many hours of editing and preparing this book for publishing.

~God Bless~

BETHANY JOYCE TEMPLE LINEAGE

William Temple m. Rebecca Tatum

William Temple, Jr. m. Elizabeth Chambliss

Henry Temple, Sr. m. Elizabeth Barker

Jesse Temple m. Unknown

Benjamin Temple m. Elizabeth Amy Wright

Lloyd Temple m. Susanna Freeman

William Rankin Temple m. Phelona Jane Young

Elijah Franklin Temple m. Mary Eliza Emmons (Underwood)

Green Irvin Temple m. Vinnie Mae Moore died giving birth.
                           m. Margaret Florene Wilson

Bethany Joyce Temple

THE TEMPLE'S

The beginning of the Temple family originated in England. At this time in history, the structure of the castle remains as Temple Hall. These early Temples were set aside for religious purposes.

In the year 1279, the Manor or Temple Hall was held by Henry DeTemple. Temple Hall was in possession of Sir Peter Temple, Lekester branch of the Temple family. At the time of Cromwell, until 1663, it was confiscated by Charles II. Sir Peter Temple and James Temple had signed the death warrant of Charles I. To this day, it is still called Temple Hall. It is in Liecester County, near the village of Sibon, England. Currently, in history, the owner of this estate is Mr. Earl Howe.

For additional information about the Temple estates and names of early Temple's, and other information, see references below.

"Our Temple Family," author Jerry Eugene Green, my first cousin, Alpha Jane Temple Green's son. She is my dad's, G.l. Temple, sister. "G.I. Temple Soldier of Faith and The Pearl," page 6.

AUTHOR
BETHANY JOYCE TEMPLE

My Family by Bethany Joyce Temple.

My parents, G. I. Temple and Margaret Florene Wilson-Temple had eight children. I am their last child. I married, and divorced Lawrence Arthur Smith and we have five children.

My children are Lawrence Dion Smith m/Heather Pyle; Sidney Lynn Smith; Tony Clay Smith m/Ashley Smith-Smith; Amy Yvette Smith m/Louis Rios; Shanara Angelle Smith m/Scott Smith.

My 11 grandchildren are Nicholas Branden Smith, Tony Clay Smith, Jr., Colton Garrett Smith, Sadie Smith, Emily Ann Smith; Moses Ian Rios, Cheyenne Nilda Rios, Angel Joyce Rios, Xavier Dexter Odamus Rios; and Richard Scott Smith, Noah Alexander Autin, Raven Amelia Coats and Luna Ashlyn Coats.

I was born July 17, 1950. My ministry is entitled "Stay Focus Messages," which consists of 62 contacts. I had written 21 gospel songs. Seventeen of them are copyrighted in the Library of Congress. My prayer is that everyone who reads this book will be ministered to spiritually and naturally. The Holy Bible is like a two-edged sword.

I AM BETHANY, CHOSEN, A SPIRITUAL WARFARE

Greetings in the name of Jesus. I greet you with love. The Holy Bible says to repent because the Kingdom of Heaven is at hand. Jesus is on His way back; it is time to prepare for the day of the Lord.

I would like to first try to get some or all my readers to understand my writing of Job's perfection and uprightness. We do not compare ourselves to another's walk with the Lord. Only God knows us. He sees us for who we are, not who I am. God is a jealous God. I am not who people say that I am in their minds. God knows all things. He knows our name. He is a righteous Judge. He judges our hearts whether we are pure and holy or wicked and evil.

The book of Job is a good example for God's children in spiritual warfare. This is what we must see in our lives from the beginning. Do not think it's strange when things come against you. We are targets for Satan's attacks. He is after you and me. Satan even tells God what he does daily, walking to and fro seeking whom he may destroy. God points us out to Satan and asks if he has considered you or me. God gives Satan permission to tempt us. He tells Satan to do all he has in his power, other than take a life. Many of God's people know personally what I am saying. There is so much pain and heart aches that we go through, but we are still holding on to God's unchanging hand.

We are not full grown in the things of God, as we were not when we came from our mother's womb. Jesus Christ,

God's only begotten Son did not arrive on this earth ready to minister. We all must grow, be taught, and learn. It takes some longer than others to excel in the wisdom, knowledge, and understanding of the Word of God. The Holy Bible says that Jesus learned obedience through the things He suffered, even to His death on the cross. We still do not compare one to another. Our children are all different. Only God knows all things.

 I remember talking to the Lord verbally telling Him I am so without understanding. I am the least to be able to minister in His Kingdom. I watched as some men or women ministered to individuals. I saw many times that the words they spoke were not from God. I would tell the Lord that I would not speak to people what He did not say. I did not want to be a fake. I wrestled with this in my mind. If the enemy would try to speak a lie from my mouth, I would speak the truth. I would say, let every man be a lie but God's Word is true. Our warfare is within our own selves, flesh fighting against the Spirit.

SATAN VISITS

I remember a very vivid dream/vision at early years of my marriage. As time went on, I continued my walk with Jesus. I saw an increase in demonic seducing spirits to full fledge abomination sex sins from the pit of hell. I have seen how the devil is after the ministers and leaders of the church and on to the Saints. He has come down to wear out the Saints of the highest God. He comes to kill, steal, and destroy. There is no good thing in him, nothing! We must not grow weary in well doing. We will reap if we faint not.

I had gone to bed for the night. The dream/vision was so real, lifelike. Soon in the darkness of night, I saw this figure who looked larger than a normal man. It was over my lower body. His legs were spread as if in a sexual position. I could not speak; it was like I was in a trance. His large hands were spread over my lower body. He began slowly to slide them over my stomach, then onto my breast. He continued slowly sliding his hands until they were around my neck and spoke with a harsh raspy voice from the pit. He began squeezing my neck. He spoke and said, "I have been wanting to do this for a long time." I awoke as I felt like warm blood was coming from my ears. I tried calling Jesus's name, but nothing came from my voice. I continued until I was saying, "The Blood of Jesus." The dark figure lost his hold on my neck and fled into the darkness.

BETHANY CHOSEN – A SPIRITUAL WARFARE – DECEPTION

The holy scripture says that Satan wants to be like God of all. He knows that God is the Most High God. Satan is a deceiver. He cannot speak the truth. He is a liar. He cannot love. He lusts. People fall for his evil deceit. Why? Because they do not know God. They cannot tell Satan's voice from God's. Why? Because they do not know God! How do you know God? Call out His name from your heart. When you call from your heart, God hears you. He will answer you. Get into His Holy Word. The Holy Bible is the written Word of God. You will learn His voice - teachings. Do not follow a stranger, the enemy, ole Satan.

Are you being deceived? Stop following men, their teachings, and their doctrines. Follow the Lord Jesus Christ. You will not be deceived! He is Truth! He is the Life; He is the Way.

I AM CHOSEN BETHANY LIKE JOB? SPIRITUAL BATTLE

Job 1:6, Now there was a day when the sons of God came to present themselves before the Lord, and Satan came also among them. There was a man (woman) in the land named Job; that man (woman) was perfect and upright; one that feared God and eschewed or shunned evil. His (her) sons feasted in their houses every day. They sent and called for their three sisters to eat and drink with them. It was so when their days of feasting were gone. Job sent and sanctified them. He rose up early in the morning and offered burnt offerings according to the number of them. Job said, "It may be that my sons have sinned and cursed God in their hearts." Thus did Job continually. Job 1:6, Now there was a day when the sons of God came to present themselves before the Lord. Satan came also among them. (v.7) The Lord said, "Whence comest thou?" Then Satan answered the Lord, saying, "From going to and fro in the earth, from walking up and down in it. (v.8) The Lord said unto Satan, "Hast thou considered my servant Job? There is none like him in the earth, a perfect and upright man or woman, one that fears God and escheweth (shuns) evil?" (v.9), Then Satan answered the Lord, and said, "Does Job fear God for naught? Has thou not made a hedge about him, about his house, and about all he has on every side? Thou hast blessed the work of his hands. His substance is increased in the land. (v.11) Put forth thy hand now and touch all that he has, and he will curse thee to thy face. (v.12) And the Lord said to Satan, "Behold all that he has is in thy power, only upon himself, put not thy hand." So, Satan went far from the presence of the Lord. (v.13) Now there came a time his sons went and feasted

BETHANY "TEMPLE OF GOD"

in their houses everyone his day. They sent and called for their three sisters to eat and drink with them in the elder brother's house. (v.14) And messengers came to Job. (v.15) The Sabeans fell upon your children and took them away. Your servants are slain. (v.16) While he was yet speaking came another messenger; fire of God is fallen from heaven. All are burnt. The sheep and servants are consumed. I am the only one left. (v.17) Another messenger came, Chaldeans fell upon your camels, took them. They have slain your servants, I only am alive. (v.18) Another came saying, "Your sons and daughters were eating and drinking wine in the eldest son's house. A great wind from the wilderness smote four corners of the house. It fell upon the young men. They are dead, I only am alive. (v.20) Job arose and rent his mantle. He shaved his head, fell on the ground, and worshipped God. (v.21) Job said, "Naked I came out of my mother's womb, naked I shall return. The Lord gave, and the Lord has taken away. Blessed be the name of the Lord." (v.22) In all this Job (woman), sinned not nor charged God foolishly.

BETHANY – NAMES HAVE MEANING

I am Bethany Joyce Temple. I was born July 17, 1950, in Richland Parish, Rayville, Louisiana. My dad is Green Irvin Temple; he was 43 years of age when I was born. My mom is Margaret Florene Wilson Temple; her mom is Mary Margaret Silva/Silvey. Mom was 41 years old when I was born. I am their 8th child. Numbers have meaning also. #8 means a new beginning. 7 means complete. 50 means Pentecost, Holy Ghost. Bethany means 8 beginning. Dad and Mom had a new beginning, Pentecost, infilling of the Holy Ghost. It was new the beginnings of G.I. Temple's and Margaret Florene's Christian life in Jesus Christ. My Bible name Bethany Joyce Temple meaning = Date House/Fruit House-family, daughter lodge within - Temple, builder any transition, obtain children, deliver, proclaim, set apart, sweet smelling, outburst of passion/Jesus. Sent, go straight away, loose, bring, say, done, spoken, prophet, saying, tell the daughter of the Sion, "Behold thy king comes". I went and did as commanded; I cry hosanna to the son of David! "Blessed is he that comes in the name of the highest." Cast out, overthrow, I was blind, lost, lame, healed lodged, Feast of Passover/unleavened bread, House of Simon the Leper, Mary, Martha, and Lazarus. Anointing, dead raised, gospel preached, memorial told communion, the blood/wine, the body, and bread. At Mount Of Olives, near Jerusalem. At even tide, Jesus Christ went and lodged. To Bethany, my house shall be called the House of prayer, but you have made it a den of thieves. Have faith in God, say do not doubt, believe, it shall come to pass. Receive, stand praying. Forgive. Indwell, host, abide, open air, to blow, sheepfold, camp down, rest, to remain guest, be strange, hospitable, encamp, occupy, to reside. God's residence Jesus Christ, to accept, to receive, a symbol of protection and communion.

Luke 24: 45-49, Jesus Christ opened their understanding, that they might understand the scriptures. He said, "It is written." It behooved Christ to suffer and to rise from the dead on the third day, that repentance and remission of sins should be preached in His name among all nations, beginning at Jerusalem. You are witnesses of these things. Behold, I send the promise of my father upon you. But tarry you in the city of Jerusalem until you are endued with power from on high. Luke 24: 50, And He led them out as far as Bethany. And He lifted up His hands and blessed them. And it came to pass, while He blessed them, He parted from them and was carried up into heaven.

BETHANY'S - TRANSITION – REVELATION

The Holy Spirit ministered to me that I shall no longer be called Becky. I shall be called Bethany. He showed me there was hidden manna inside of me. I was blessed to be alerted to hear what God wanted to speak to me. You see, I was in a spiritual battle. I was trying to lean on my own wisdom, knowledge, and understanding. I knew that I needed to call on my God for His wisdom, knowledge, and understanding. I went through this spiritual warfare that attacked my mind, body, soul, and spirit. Thank God for preparing me for what I have been going through, and more so now. Back in 2007, even until now, God put anointing in my daily life. There is power in prayer, fasting, and anointing with His Holy blessed oil. Just within our own flesh, we are weak. We need help. God is always with us and helps us.

We must prepare for warfare ourselves. We must put on the whole armor of God to fight the enemy. We as Christians must get the understanding that God is not going to do it all. We must do our part! We must get understanding that God wants His power to flow through each person. This power will flow to our family, friends, and whosoever we pray for. We need the power of the Holy Spirit, deliverances, healings, miracles, and salvation that come in Jesus' name. We are overcomers! Revelation 2:17 states, "He that has an ear, let him hear, what the Spirit says to the church. To him that overcomes I will give to eat of the hidden mana; I will give him a white stone; in the stone, a new name written, which no man knoweth saving he that receiveth it," … "Bethany."

BETHANY'S TRANSITION - DESTINY

Psalms 90: 10 says, the days of our years are three score years, 70; and 10 = 80 years, if by reason of strength, health, they be 4 score years = 80. Yet it is their strength labor, and sorrow, for it is soon cut off, and we will fly away. This is a journey I have been on since my year 71, 2021. Both numbers and with the number one, which means a new beginning. I have fulfilled my years from scripture, Psalm 90:10. Now I am over, to a new beginning of a period, as God's will, purpose, and plan for my life, my destiny.

WHO IS BETHANY?
MY DAUGHTER RAISED FROM DEAD

John 1:11-13, Jesus came to His own and His own received Him not. As many as received Him, to them He gave power to become sons or daughters of God. He gave to them that believe on His name; which were not born of blood, nor of the will of the flesh, nor of the will of man, but of God!!!

Bethany was God's chosen name for me. Jesus' meaning lodge, God's daughter, God's Temple, Bethany transitions, Bethany obtain children, deliver, proclaim set apart, sweet smelling savor, an outburst of passion! Jesus sent prophets saying, "Tell the daughter of Zion saying, behold thy king comes, repent for the Kingdom of heaven is at hand, prepare for the day of the Lord"!! I went. I did as commanded.

"I cry Hosanna to the son of David; blessed is He that comes in the name of the highest." I have cast out demon spirits through the name and blood of Jesus Christ. God has used me to make known of evil spirits inside the House of God. God could no longer go into His own house! It was a stink in His nostrils. Jesus said, "My house shall be called the House of Prayer, you have made it a den of thieves." My own daughter was raised from the dead. She was in the Hospice three times, due to her low immune system. She would get so weak and have no strength or appetite. Prayers went forth for her. I was sitting in her room waiting for her to pass. The Holy Spirit stirred me. He asked me why I was sitting there just waiting and watching. I went to her bed and picked her up like a rag doll; she was so lightweight.

I sat her in the recliner next to the bed. She could not sit up. Daily I would get her out of the bed and put her in the chair. I fed her as strength began to return to her body. She was able to hold her head up. Thank God for her life!!!

When she was released from Hospice, she was excited, ready to get out of the house. Like a free bird, she got into her vehicle and was gone. Two men from Hospice came to get their supplies. One of the men went into the house starting to remove the bed and supplies. The second man stood outside under the carport for me to sign papers as each item was removed from the house. He began to let me know how sorry he was for my loss. I said, "It's all right, we did not lose anybody." He said, "Yes, but this was expected." He was glad how I was strong with my loss. Again, I said to him that we did not lose anyone. The first man spoke up to the one that I was with. He said, "Did you see that lady leaving in the van when we drove up?" The second man said yes he did. The first one said, "That's the lady who was on Hospice." This man I've been talking with spoke up surprised, and said, "You have got to be kidding!" Thank God for victory over death, hell, and the grave! I am not a prophet. I'm not a preacher or a pastor. I am just a daughter of God! He has used me in several areas of ministry, all praise, honor, and glory to my Father God! I love God, Jesus, Holy Spirit with all my heart, mind, body, soul, and spirit. I love my neighbor as myself; all nations, creed and colors. Have faith in God. Do not doubt. Believe and it shall come to pass. Just receive. Stand praying, forgiving.

WHO IS BETHANY? FIGHTING DEMONS

This same daughter went through so much abuse in her young life. She experienced molestation. She married into drug abusive lifestyle. I had never gone through so much abuse as my child did. My children were raised in church. They were targets for the enemy. Believe me that he did a number on them! But thank God for the remnant of elder family Christians. We know how to pray. We know what it takes to put that serpent's head under our feet and crush him. One day my daughter was low, frail, and seemed hopeless. I was called to go pick up her and the children. Their dad was already picked up and locked up. I brought them to my house. I was washing dishes when my daughter came up to me. She began talking to me, asking who I was. I knew something was wrong with her. I knew evil spirits were present. I spoke to her. I told her that I was Bethany Temple, her mother. She said, oh, you must be Helena. She was relating my Temple name to the Knights Templars from England's history. I had not eaten, but God knows all things. He knew that Satan and his demons would show up. There's power in fasting, praying, and anointing oil, pleading the blood of Jesus to spiritual warfare. She then went into the bedroom. I heard her crying, "Daddy, Daddy, Daddy." I went into the room. She had her arms crossed like hugging, crying, "Daddy." I went up to her and said, "No, it's Jesus, Jesus, Jesus." She repeated me saying, "Jesus, Jesus, Jesus." I said, "Yes, Jesus." She began to choke. I prayed with the blood of Jesus. She began spitting and slobbering. I knew demons were acting up against the name of Jesus. I got my anointing olive oil. I anointed the door posts and overhead of all the doors with the blood of Jesus. I anointed my daughter.

The demons began to speak. They said, "Stop, that burns." As I pleaded the blood of Jesus, I commanded the evil spirits to come out. She began to twist and turn, pulling, withdrawing, and backing away. She was weak from those spirits coming out. She began speaking in another evil sounding tone. I started asking the spirits what their names were. Each one answered their name as I would call that demon by name and commanded him to come out. Hours passed as these demons had to obey and come out. The spirits of pornography, adultery, drugs, alcohol, sex spirits-Succubus, and Incubus, filthy nasty sexual spirits. My body was getting tired and weak commanding, casting the demons out.

I called for help, praying against all those demons. I thought of several people, including my cousin, Pastor Roger Temple. He was overseas in Saudi Arabia. I called local people. Some were afraid of demons; some people just would not come. The Holy Spirit spoke to me to call Brother Jimmy Sims. It was a couple of hours after the midnight hour. I called Brother Sims' number. He answered the phone. He said that he was walking the floor. He was waiting for a call. He did not know who or what. I told him about my daughter and the demons. He began speaking in an unknown tongue and commanding the evil spirits to come out. I held the phone to her ear. He ministered to her until she went to the bathroom.

My middle son was in bed resting from staying up all night. My girl came out of the bathroom and went out the front door. She began smearing her feces on the doorposts. I got my son up and showed him what she was doing. He asked her why she did that. She said that she was anointing the door. I filled him in on what was going on. He talked her into going to the hospital. We were waiting in the examining room, and as she began choking and spitting. I spoke to the spirit and asked who he was, and he said that he was "Legion." I said I knew you were because you were many and you are coming out, too. I plead the blood of Jesus and cast them out.

BETHANY'S BEGINNINGS

I was in God's thoughts, His mind before I was conceived in my mother's womb, before I was born. I was born to serve the Lord. I was born for God's will, God's purpose, and God's plan, not for my parents, and not my own! I was chosen by God, as all chosen ones are! Although it took me a long time to catch on, to understand the will of God! The Bible says that we look in a glass darkly, then face to face. We see our journey as though through dark glass, not clear, until we get understanding. The Holy Bible says we know in part, and we prophecy in part, until that one who is perfect, "the Holy Spirit" comes. Then shall we know and understand clearly. When He comes, He moves in us, the children of the Most High God. He is from God. He knows all things.

I was a very quiet, bashful child until I was grown and working. My parents were new babies in Jesus Christ, in the Holy Spirit. We both were new babies together, them with the Holy Spirit and me, just born in the natural birth. I thought maybe if I had told Mom and Dad what I experienced, I may have been more focused and able to understand dreams, visions, thoughts, daydreams. Maybe growing up I would not have been labeled stubborn or rebellious. I do not excuse anything I may have done wrong. The scripture says when I was a child, I spoke as a child. When I am grown, I put off childish things. As we grow, we learn and understand. The Holy Spirit is our teacher. He teaches us what He hears our heavenly father speak and His son Jesus Christ. Let every man be a lie, but God's word is true. The Holy Spirit is my teacher. When I cry out, He hears my voice. He answers according to His will. I do know that the things we go through are to make us strong. We live by faith believing and knowing all things will work together for those who love God, those who are the called, and chosen for His purpose.

The Holy Spirit leads, guides, and directs our footsteps, one step at a time. We are walking by faith in Jesus's footsteps. Our steps seem slow at times. Walking in Jesus's footsteps seem slow, but they are sure steps. When He arrives, He is always on time. He is never late.

We must stay focused on the perfect one, the perfect teacher, Jesus Christ. Too many people take their focus off Him. I have seen people idolize personalities. When they fall, they all fall. The Holy Word tells us that if the blind follow the blind leader, they will both fall into the ditch together. We have oppositions and hindrances that come from the enemy, Satan. There are many voices who tickle the ears of the people. They are wolves in sheep's clothing, to lead God's leaders and people astray. I know of ministers who were Holy Spirit leaders. They heard the voice of God and walked in Him. They stopped following God's voice. They joined familiar spirits, doctrines of devils, and man's teaching which brought about confusion. The congregation split in different directions, scattered without a shepherd, and became prey to every beast of the fields. People, let us stay focused on the one, the only creator of our lives, our souls. He knows us and has everything good from above to give His children, us.

BETHANY IS IN GOD'S SPOKEN AND WRITTEN WORD

God's Word is the only true word of prophecy. His Word comes to pass in the Holy Bible. His Word continues, repeating again. It is God telling us beforehand, what happens at the beginning, repeats again. This is what we are living, a repeat. There is nothing new under heaven! God's Spoken and Written Word continues until the end of our lives on the earth. Our lives in the heavenly Kingdom realm and the dead souls in the realm of hell is the end on earth. Examples are people, characters in the Holy Bible, and other people through generations playing the same part. Unto the end of the Holy Bible, the spoken and written word of God who spoke the world, creation, into existence. This is what happens with individuals, our dreams, visions, thoughts, have happened before and now happens with us. Every person in God's creation has dreams, visions, and thoughts. These are in us from God's creation. We know of many leaders who have followed the role and characteristics of good, and evil leaders. Even in our own time, now, we see men and women play out what has happened in history, are now the people doing the same things. It's like watching an old movie again, just different people playing the actors, their same parts. Our president we had in 2017, has been playing and is still playing the part. He has not conceded his presidency. He was put into office by God, chosen! He is president, and the other evil ones are trying to continue. It is God's will, plan, and purpose to keep this satanic antichrist from making his move, trying to take over the earth. God's plan has slowed down the enemy's progress in bringing on the End Times. It is not Satan's time to deceive with his evil beast system, called the "Mark of the Beast." When time comes, God will allow him to do his evil for a short time.

    This is what has been happening now, so many are not awake, not alert. Jesus told the disciples in the garden, when they were asleep, to watch and pray, as He prayed and cried to the Father. His sweat became like great drops of blood. Sleep on!!! Then the evil ones came upon them. This is just like what will happen as the man of sin comes upon the sleepers.

|BETHANY'S BIRTHDAY MEANING 7-17-1950

My birthday, 7 means rest. In the Bible, also 17. 6 equal days God created everything, and on the 7th day, he rested from his labors. 1950 = 50, Pentecost, Filling with the Holy Ghost. During this period, Dad and Mom were filled with the Holy Ghost. I was just born, a newborn baby. Mom and Dad were just born again in the Holy Spirit; Christians, living a new life in Jesus Christ's teachings. They were no longer following the desires of the flesh. They we're following in Jesus's steps, pleasing God. I am Mom and Dad's 8th child. The number 8 means new beginning. It was a new beginning for them, as I was their new beginning child, number 8. I am living the New Beginning in my life, also.

This was The New Beginning for the entire Temple family!

G.I. and Margaret Temple were not raised in church. They were not indoctrinated with man's doctrines, teaching, and beliefs. They got into the Holy Bible and learned God's doctrines, God's commandments, Jesus Christ's teachings. Because Jesus ascended into Heaven and sent back the Holy Spirit, He taught Mom and Dad. The Word says that you need no man to teach you. The Holy Spirit Himself will teach, lead, and guide us in all truth. Mom and Dad were taught by the Teacher, himself, the Holy Spirit. He gave them gifts of the spirit, gifts of faith, miracles, tongues, and interpretations. The Holy Word says without faith it is impossible to please God. Faith is always now. Pray believing and you shall receive!

BETHANY GOES BLIND

It was the last of winter 1951 – 1952, just before spring. Dad had the fire built up warm and cozy in our old wood farmhouse. Our cast iron heater was doing its job! He kept the ashes pan pushed under the heater out of the way, but on this day, the fire Ash Pan was not under the heater all the way. I was a toddler, following my cat; my foot tripped and my face went down into the hot ashes. You can imagine my screaming! Dad and Mom were not far away. Mom softly cleaned my face. She and Dad immediately sent up prayers to our Great Physician, Jesus Christ. They got the word out to ministers and praying elders of the Body of Christ. Brother Jesse Eppinett was a good friend and pastor full of the Holy Ghost. I know God used him in ministering to Dad and Mom, as they were babes in Christ. He gave Dad a place in his church, a different demonization than the one that Dad was saved in. Dad became a member of the church where he was saved. Dad fasted and prayed! That works every time! Dad's fasting and praying get God's attention. After three days of fasting and praying, my eyes were healed like they were before the accident! I was not taken to the doctor; I did not get any medicine. My Miracle Healer, Jesus Christ, gets all praise and glory! I remember the older children telling of Dad's famous words. The children came home from school. They gathered around him as he told them what happened to my eyes. He said if they hugged and loved each other, God would heal little Becky's eyes in three days. The children said that they would obey. They hugged and told each other they loved each one. Dad obeyed God; the children obeyed Dad. We are a close family to this day. We forgive and we love. God is love!

BETHANY IS GONE – LOST IN A TORNADO

Just a couple of months following my accident of falling into the cast iron Heater ash pan, that blinded my eyes, a cyclone/tornado touched down. In May 1952, it picked our house up and sat it down in the cotton field. The family was gathered in the living room when Mom heard a roaring sound. She opened the door and saw the storm heading right to our house. As she turned around to close the door and go inside, it hit her foot. The tornado was there! As the house settled and the storm passed, Dad began to count heads to account for everybody. Everyone was accounted for except for me. Dad already had the family praying for my return. As Dad searched, he noticed that the end of the house where I was sleeping was no longer there! After his first search for me, he stopped in the living room to let everyone know that he had not found me. The family got serious, praying for my safety and safe return. Dad searched again through the house, looking under overturned furniture. He went into the living room, again and prayers went up to our Heavenly Father. Dad went outside as the worst of the storm had passed. He searched as well as he could, with lightning flashing and debris scattered over the ground.

Dad went back into the house, telling how they needed to cry out to God, to bring me back. As they were praying, crying out to God, a flash of lightning lit up the living room. Someone cried out, "There's little Becky"!! Sure enough, there I was standing beside Mom, holding onto her dress tail. An Angel of the Lord came with the flash of lightning and delivered me to my mom and family. Oh, what praising, singing, and shouting came forth unto our King of Kings and Lord of Lords, our Father God of all creation. We had an old trunk where Mom found dry clothes for me.

BETHANY'S YOUNG LIFE: VISIONS - DREAMS -THOUGHTS

I guess I was a strange, odd child from the beginning. I saw things before they happened or came to pass. That is called Foreknowledge. It is God's Kingdom coming to individuals to His chosen ones that He wants to use on the earth to spread His Gospel. He shows them beforehand in dreams, visions, and thoughts, confirming to them that they are chosen. God backs up His chosen ones as they minister to certain ones. It is His message to them that nobody knows about that person except God and the person.

Just from the two incidents in my young life showed me, at some time later, that I was a chosen vessel to be used by God. For instance, the blind eyes that God restored my sight, and the storm that blew me away, and the Angel of the Lord returned me unharmed.

I did not understand what was happening. I've heard people talk about Deja' vu. They said it meant "to see something before it happens"! Hearing that expression did not clear up anything for me. I did not understand.

I was a young teen when a friend of the family bought a pretty gift box of silk handkerchiefs and gave them to me. I was puzzled because I saw as if I had seen this before. Again, the friend bought me a comb, mirror, brush dresser set. I had seen this before as I did the gift box of handkerchiefs; I was puzzled! I did not tell anyone. I just kept it to myself. I have seen people, and places that I've not known when I saw them before. It was confusing. See how slow I am to understand.

At school I would stare out the windows. I would daydream instead of paying attention to the teachers in elementary school. I know my thoughts were not on classroom work. Maybe this is why I was referred to as stubborn or rebellious. Those words mean deliberate, does not obey instructions. God knows my heart; we should not label people with our understanding. God knows all these things. God knows our heart and God knows our name. People labeled my grandson who has autism as being stubborn and or deliberate.

I thank God that He knows me. He chose me and uses me from time to time for His kingdom. I'm honored to suffer for righteousness. I wished I would have understood His ways years ago. I would've gotten more done for the kingdom.

I grew up in the natural thinking I was to get married and raise a family. I should have searched out the scriptural things of God. That is war of the flesh with the spirit. There is a time and season for everything under the heavens, to every purpose in the plan of God. We will rest if we get into God's season, will, plan, and purpose for our lives and obey. Be encouraged, those of you who understand that you were born to serve the Lord, to do His will and not yours. You seek Him. You will find Him when you seek with all your heart. He will teach, lead, and guide you in all truths for the salvation of your family. Walk slowly and surely in His footsteps. Consider the word, the Holy Bible, and what He says about our Lord and Savior. Luke 2:40-52, The child Jesus grew and waxed strong in spirit. Filled with wisdom; and the grace of God was upon Him. Every year His family went to

Jerusalem at the Feast of Passover. When He was 12 years old, they went to Jerusalem after the custom of the feast. (The Temples went to camp meeting yearly, also family reunion.) When the days were fulfilled, He stayed behind. After three days, they found Jesus sitting in the midst of the doctors, hearing them and asking questions. All that heard Him were astonished at His understanding and answers. He told His parents that He must be about His Heavenly Father's business. Jesus went home with them and was subject unto them. 52, Mary kept all Jesus' sayings in her heart. Jesus increased in wisdom and stature and found favor with God and man. Luke 3, John was shut into prison, 21, Jesus was baptized being 30 years of age, full of the Holy Ghost, began His ministry. Age has no restrictions to God's will in our life.

When I was older in my life, my children were in high school. Brother Foster was our pastor in Venice, Louisiana at the time. He called me to the front of the church, and he gave the word of knowledge of prophecy to me. As he began, he called me "Daughter of Zion"; he saw me in the spirit. He saw me up on a high mountain. My hair and dress were blowing in the wind. He saw jagged rocks all around where I was standing. The enemy was all around hoping to watch me fall. He said God was going to use me mightily.

Later my oldest son was in the 12th grade, and I had my fifth child. There was lots of turmoil in my marriage. I went with a church lady friend to New Orleans. She told me that the pastor was used in "Word of Knowledge and Prophecy." I went through the prayer line as the others did. I have never been there. I had never seen them in person. The pastor minister spoke to me as the Holy Ghost spoke to her, and revealed to her things I was going through. I know that she was close to God and He did show her the things about me.

I had never been to that building where she was. When I walked in and looked around, I saw this place as I had in the spirit, a vision. Even my older daughter's first time going, saw it looked familiar to her. It was not a regular church building, matter of fact, it was the old Mason Strip Street Bar. That is the kind of change the Lord likes, not to turn the church into a bar but to turn the bar into the church, take from Satan and make him angry. Many souls were being served ,and Holy Ghost filled, healed, and delivered from satanic possession. There was a new Holy Ghost dance and under the influence of the Holy Spirit, New Wine. The lady preacher referred to me as the messenger of God. The messenger gives out the message that was given to them, that's all, nothing added to and nothing less, nothing taken away.

As a child, when I went to church, I would leave as soon as the service was over. I did not stand around and talk or gossip. I always do this when I visit family or friends. I said, I know when to hold them; I know when to fold them; I know when to walk away; I know when to run. We do not have to participate in things or conversations that bother our spirit, if we do not want to take part in these things, that cause conflict, gossip, or to anger people. It is better for us to flee, run. God is not pleased and idle talk that brings about strife and contention. God is not author of confusion. The Holy Spirit gave men or women of God that spoke to me words of wisdom, words of knowledge, words of understanding as I transitioned from one stage in my life to the next. I thank God for the real man and women of God who pay the price to be close to our Master. God trusts these people with information for another child of God.

God showed me that He is a jealous God. I cannot have anyone or anything that I put before God. A lot of my problems, our problems, are not always about someone else. Sometimes God allows things and people to be part of our discomfort, so that God can take us in another direction in our life. My symptoms are usually miserable, lonely, sad, and uncertain about what's next for my life. I was void, worthless, not fitting in. As I broke down, my will broke, now God could work with me and in me. I found God's will in my life. He began to lead, guide, direct my path, and show me His way to go. I now have understanding and direction in my life as I stay focused on Jesus. It is not for others to understand what God is doing for you or for me. As long as I walk one step at a time in Jesus's footsteps, I will stay on the right path for me. His steps are slow, but they are sure

BETHANY ON THE FARM

My family owns a 60-acre farm. Cotton was our money crop, white gold. It paid our bills, our entire family worked together to keep our farm producing. You heard the saying that a family that prays together stays together. That is our G.I. Temple and Margaret Florene Wilson Temple family.

I remember my first job with my Temple family. It was in the 'cotton fields of home'. I was the water girl who took the bucket of water with the dipper that everybody drank from. Those rows of cotton seemed so tall as I stepped from one to the other. Water sloshed with every row I crossed until I reached them. My family were blessed that I got to them with any water for them to drink. Now the hoe tool was my next job in the cotton fields. I was to help thin the cotton and cut grass out. When we finished all the acres of cotton and cutting grass, we would start again. We continued this until almost July 4. We had to get out of the cotton field so we would not disturb the plants as they produced. We were happy for July 4, Independence Day! We got 'independent' and had a day of fun. We went swimming, fishing, making homemade ice cream, and ate lots of watermelons. Yummy! Fun time was over too soon! Now the cotton bolls had made, and opened showing the bright white cotton. It was cotton picking time. Mom had cotton sacks for us to put our cotton in, as we pulled it from the burr. The sack strap went over our head and on our shoulder. The sack was pulled behind us on the ground as our hands picked the cotton putting it in the opening of the sack. When the cotton sack was full, we threw the sack over our shoulder and carried it to the scales to be weighed.

Our scale was on a tree branch. A pee weight was used to weigh the cotton. The cotton was then emptied into a long trailer with sides. When the trailer was full, it had to be pulled to the cotton gin. There was a large suction hose put over the picked cotton and sucked into the gin building. The cotton was pressed, the seeds were separated from the cotton. The cotton seeds were planted with a planter behind the Mule, then by the tractor later. I remember when I was young, playing jumping on the cotton in the back of the trailer. Dad told me to get out. He did not want the fluffy cotton packed down. I did not get out. I do not know if I was not paying attention or why I did not get out! My dad gave me a whipping. Back in those days, they told you one time to do something. They put the switch or belt to your behind the next time. To obey is better than sacrifice. Ouch! Lesson learned!

BETHANY – THE GARDEN

We worked in our vegetable garden. There was much work to do on the farm. We planted seeds; also, set out vegetable plants. The plants were peppers, onions, and tomatoes. Our seed vegetables were corn, beans, peas, okra, and others. The seed vegetables were watered by the rain and dew. We had to take buckets of water to water the plants. God's sunshine and rain helped with all the garden plants. The vegetables had to be gathered at harvest time. We had to shell the peas and beans. We had big metal tubs full of picked vegetables. We would sit under a shade tree or on the porch, sometimes in the house, shelling and singing gospel songs.

The vegetables were rinsed in clean water and prepared for canning. We put some in glass jars, and others were put into freezer bags. We ate fresh vegetables in season. Those put into jars and into the freezer were for other months. When family and friends came to visit or stay a while, we always had plenty of food. My, my! Some good eating!

We had chickens for the eggs and meat. We had pigs for pork, meat and cows for the milk and butter and beef. We had good eating on the farm. I helped churn the milk for butter. Oh yes, we had rich cow milk with delicious thick cream that rose to the top. That was our coffee mate! This thick, rich cream made the best pies, cakes, cookies, frosting, and the best fudge! Yummy!

BETHANY – THE BARNYARD

I did not like to go to the barnyard. Why? Because the animals would come running thinking that I had something for them to eat. I was afraid that they would rush towards me, and I would fall. They are not usually aggressive; they all just come to you at the same time. That is not good for safety reasons. Mom would send me to the barn to get corn and Irish potatoes to take back to the house. That middle section of the barn is where certain vegetables lasted longer when spread out, for example, potatoes and onions. They also would have the fresh taste of just picked vegetables. The floor was raised up higher from the ground. Sometimes there were chicken snakes between the cracks of the boards. I guess they had their bellies full of birds and chicken eggs. I did not bother them. They did not bother me.

The problem I had was that, now, I was afraid to leave the barn! The barn door was open. All the animals were gathering in the doorway blocking my way out. I had to throw some ears of corn out the door as far as my arms could. The animals ran to the food. I had to work fast. I had to carry the bucket of potatoes and corn, as well as close the door behind me. They ate those few ears of corn fast. My legs ran to the fence, opening it. I had to carefully get my legs over the hot wire fence without getting shocked. Thank God for his strength that I was safe on my way to the house and would not get a switching. My mom was watchful! Mom knew the obstacles that I had to get through.

BETHANY – FREE LUNCH

I did not care about school. I did not like to leave home. I was shy and school was full of strangers. I felt safe and secure on our 60-acre farm and going to church. All children were quiet and respectful back in my day. Today they are not. The gym was a playroom, square dance room, and candy room. I remember the first time that I ate a pretzel. They were tiny stick type treats with salt sprinkles. They were all straight, and they were in a square, rectangle, cardboard box. A friend bought a box and gave me some. They look like tiny sticks of wood with salt sprinkles. I was cautious about putting one in my mouth. I decided to try it. Wow, I never thought a stick of wood could taste so good! Yes, I did try a tiny stick that looked like the pretzel! Yuck! It was not the same!

We had free meals at school. Most of the farmers' children did receive free lunch. The small farmers, especially, who did not get a large income with their a few acres of cotton. The principal must have had a bad day at school one day. We had to walk to the office to receive our lunch card. Remember, I was already shy. When the principal looked up and saw this little poor farmer's daughter come in for her card, he had to say something smart. He talked like the food was coming out of his pocket. Tears came to my eyes; I was so embarrassed. It was still fresh on my mind when I got home. I told Dad what happened at school and the remark the principal made. My dad went to school and reminded the principal that the farmers are the hard workers, and we pay our taxes. That school lunch card did not come from his pocket.

BETHANY'S NEW BIRTH AT SNAKE RIDGE CHURCH OF GOD

It was 1958, and I was eight years of age, yes, the eighth is new beginning of my new birth. My oldest brother, John Temple, was the pastor of the Snake Ridge Church of God. We were in a Holy Ghost revival. The Holy Ghost fire from the Holy Spirit broke out and spread throughout the community. People around this rural community came out to see what the fire was all about. They found out when that fire got on them! They began to shout, dance, and scream as a new language came forth from their mouths. People were healed of sicknesses and diseases, and many more were delivered from evil spirits and set free from Satan's bondage of sin. God heard the cries of the people and Brother John Temple was chosen to come. The chosen obey. Many are called but few are chosen. Our own Temples were blessed in that very out of the way community. My sister Diane was filled with the Holy Ghost at the age of 12; my brother, Boyce, and Hilda, my niece, were 10. My nephew Keith was nine. My niece Lynette, another nephew Larry, and myself were eight years of age.

There was a large family who lived nearby just across the bridge behind the church. I don't know how many of them, and others who are Holy Ghost filled, God knows. The Cochran's were the large family. I remember an older girl, I guess in her late teens. Her name was Yvonne Stevens. She sang so beautifully, with a strong voice. I remember two songs she sang that I liked and learned. The songs were "Wait A Little Longer, Please Jesus," and "I've Got More Than My Share," good memories, good friends, good church.

That little old wood country church where my siblings and I received the Holy Ghost, reminds me of an old country gospel song that I heard several years ago. My brother John Temple was a pastor, a preacher, he was a missionary to Nicaragua. My dad, Reverend G. I. Temple, was a preacher/evangelist. He was an old-time preacher. He was a simple man with a third-grade education. (Back in his day was farming, cotton and vegetables that paid their bills and kept the family fed and clothed.) He preached the gospel of Jesus Christ so simply; the child could understand.

I remember as a child, in that little church long ago, as children were praying, singing, and shouting; we were seeking for the Holy Ghost. While we were kneeling at the altar, tears came streaming down. The Holy Spirit moved right in and filled us with the Holy Ghost; speaking and other tongues. I remember the last time I heard my daddy pray. He knelt and bowed low to the floor. He said to me, if we never meet again this side of heaven, I want to see you on the other shore. If you want to receive this precious Holy Ghost, He is a gift that comes from God. He will help to keep you strong. He will teach, lead, and guide you as you walk each step you take. He will help you be a witness as you go along your way.

I believe after the infilling of the Holy Ghost, is when the Temple sisters began learning and singing special songs at churches, and camp meetings. Remember, I said how bashful I was? I really was nervous as we got before congregations to sing. There were four of us, my sister Diane, my two nieces, Hilda and Lynette, and myself. I enjoyed singing unto the Lord, especially, when the Holy Ghost anointing came upon us. We were in the spirit and not aware of all the faces looking at us. Then there came a time when we got older, the other three got part-time jobs after school. My oldest niece got married first. Finally, I was left standing alone to sing. Now, I was truly getting scared and nervous. I had a dad that believed everyone must do their part. The special singing had to continue. I was the one left standing, so I did my part. In the late 50s in the 60s, the Holy Spirit moved with power. The guitar players, the piano and other musicical instruments had a voice of their own, loud! I got a tambourine. It was a help to me. My thoughts/mind got off people as I played the tambourine and sang. My nervous body would calm down. The Holy Ghost took over as the people shouted and danced in the spirit. The more I minister to the people, the Holy Ghost ministers to me. I flowed from that moment. I still get some butterflies when I get up before people at churches and camp meetings. But I do my part!

BETHANY'S PRETEEN YEARS
SOUTH OF THE TRACKS

I remember there was a small church in the country, south of the tracks. Dad and some of us children would fellowship occasionally. This one certain time, Dad was asked to bring the message. That night I was choked up with a cold. I was Dad's special guest singer. My voice surely was not up to singing a special song. Just before Dad went up to preach the sermon, he called me up to the platform. I tried to get his attention by saying that I could not sing. Dad cannot hear my voice. I went up on the platform. The people were already singing, shouting, and praising God. Nobody heard as I tried to excuse myself. The music was already playing, and my mouth opened. They did not realize that only every other word was coming out. Wow! Nowadays, the shouting, praising, and worship has come to an end. Nobody can get by singing like that now unless the guitars are out of tune or rhythm, nor don't know the song. I have learned when you get up to sing just let the anointing take over and God will do the rest. The true worshipers will make the difference.

BETHANY'S PRETEEN – TRIP TO VIRGINIA

I remember a trip that Dad (G.I. Temple), Mom (Margaret Florene Wilson Temple), and I went on. It was way, far from our Louisiana 60-acre farm. This trip that I'm talking about was to the great state of Virginia. My brother Jim D. Temple was a soldier in the army. Jim met his wife, Darlene Jenkins, while stationed in Virginia. Boyce had bought a brand-new green truck for Dad. (By the way, Green is what the G stands for in Dad's name.) He also bought a camper shell that he securely attached to it. With our large temple family, you know Mom and Dad did not leave without a load of us children. I was in Junior High School. It was exciting to tell my school friends about our trip to our Capitol of the USA. Boyce was Dad's help with driving over many miles. He of course, rode up front in the cab of the truck with Mom and Dad. There were several children in the back. Let me try to remember each one that rode in the back of the truck. I was one of five: Lonnie, Roger, B. B. (Byron) and Keith. We had a mattress and quilts to sit on. We had some comfort for when we had bumpy roads.

Mom and Dad brought plenty of water and snacks to eat and drink. We stopped several times off-road at rest areas. It was a long trip. It seemed like we would never arrive at Jim and Darlene's home. We did not realize what we looked like until we arrived at Jim's home. As each one got out of the truck, my sister-in-law looked surprised! I do believe one thing, she was counting heads. She was probably thinking, where would she find that many beds for that many people to sleep. There were eight Temple kinfolks that piled from that truck. We probably look like some Beverly Hillbillies. The three people from the cab were adults. The five in the back we're children. Darlene's dad and mother, Brother and Sister Jenkins blessed us with places to sleep and delicious food to eat. They had no grandbabies at that time. But let me say, God has blessed the Temple/Jenkins family with a multitude! This is biblical! My brother James DeVonne Temple Senior has the fourth generation of James DeVonne Temple Junior, James DeVonne Temple the third, and James DeVonne Temple the fourth. This is not an accident, incident nor coincidence. This is a witness, a testimony to God's Holy Bible, His word is true. The promise God gave to our forefathers; Abraham, Isaac, and Jacob!!! Dad was blessed to speak to a large congregation. He gave testimonies of some of the miracles that took place in his ministry. The word of God says that our gifts will make room for us. God does just want He says! Always! He never fails! I, Bethany Joyce Temple, love my Lord my God with all of my heart, mind, body, soul, and spirit. I also love my neighbor as myself.

BETHANY, DAD, & KEITH

Bethany, Dad (G. I. Temple), and John Keith were invited to Morgan City for a couple of nights' revival. They had heard about the gifts of miracles, healing, and wonders that God performed in this man of God. This was a large church. It did not have the people according to the capacity it could hold. But those who came were hungry for the word of God. Reverend G. I. Temple flowed with the gospel of Jesus Christ. He also exhorted the people. He preached the gifts of healing, miracles, and wonders. Those who came believed the word. Many people were saved and delivered of demonic spirits. Some of the people were filled with the Holy Ghost. People were healed of sicknesses and ailments. John Keith and I were the special singers for the Reverend G. I. (Irvin) Temple. There was a certain young lady at the same revival who was filled with the Holy Ghost. This was in the mid-1960s, my preteen years.

In the year 2020, I met the same lady who was filled with the Holy Ghost in the Morgan City revival! Do you know how God works? This was the word of the Lord being confirmed. I was at our Temple family church one Sunday morning. I was asked to sing a song. The Lord has been revealing certain scriptures to me. Often when I read the book of Daniel, chapters 10 and 11 King James, I would feel that God wanted to reveal to me something significant instead of singing. I told the congregation that I wanted to share the word of God. I told them how God was dealing with me about Daniel 11:1-4. I read the Scriptures as I revealed to them what God revealed to me.

GOD CONFIRMING HIS WORD

In the book of Ezra 1:1, now and this first year of Cyrus king of Persia, that the word of the Lord by the mouth of Jeremiah might be fulfilled. The Lord stirred up the spirit of Cyrus King of Persia. He made a proclamation throughout all his kingdom. He put into writing saying King Cyrus of Persia, "the Lord has given to me all the kingdoms of earth. He has charged me to build Him a house at Jerusalem". In the book of Ezra, Trump, President of the United States of America, is compared to King Cyrus. Israel made a coin with King Cyrus on one side, the other side of the coin was President Trump. Their comparison was what Ezra 1:1 tells us. At the beginning of the Trump administration, President Trump told the world that the first thing when he was elected, he would declare Jerusalem the eternal Capitol of Israel. President Trump declared Jerusalem the eternal Capitol of Israel. He also had put it into writing.

We are in cycles of the Bible. What was is now! What has been is now! The Holy Bible is the living word of God. It is true. The same things happened again throughout our time. There are different characters, but the same story repeating itself. There is nothing déjà vu, everything has happened before and continues a cycle. This is the holy word of God! This is the living true word of God! I've read the word of God; I read Daniel 10 and 11:1-4. I never heard prophets nor ministers explain or minister on these words. Darius the Mede represents President Trump. In the first year of Darius the Mede, President Trump, Daniel 11:1-4 says, "I Michael the Angel "stood to confirm Daniel and to strengthen him. Now I show you the truth, is the divided kingdom (America and Israel). The divided kingdom, the two legs are the Medes and the Persians (the Republicans and the Democrats). Verse 2 is talking about King Darius the Mede/Trump. "Now I will show you the truth. There shall yet stand up three kings in Persia/America. The fourth, Donald Trump, shall be far richer than they all. By his strength, through his riches, he shall stir up all against the realm of Greece. President Donald John Trump is the first of American presidents to be far richer than they all. He cannot be bought. He cannot be bribed. He will not be a puppet. By his strength through his riches, he shall stir up all against the realm of Greece. President Donald John Trump is this man! Verse 3, A mighty king shall stand up, that shall rule with great dominion, and do according to his will, (not God's will; his will is for vengeance). Verse 4, and when he shall stand up, his kingdom shall be broken, and shall be divided toward the four winds of heaven; and not to his posterity, nor according to his dominion which he ruled; (not to his kin, family) for his kingdom shall be plucked up (the Eagle, America), even for others beside those. Read verse 5 and the rest of the story, Daniel 11:1- 45 and chapter 12.

Also, I believe that soon, we are coming close to the last President of the United States. When this happens, we are that close to the man of sins being made known, also, and The Church going up to meet our Lord in the air!

DANIEL 10 AND 11 & LAST AMERICAN PRESIDENT?

He shall stand up, and shall rule with great dominion, and do according to his will. When he shall stand up, his kingdom shall be broken and divided toward the four winds of heaven. Not to his prosperity, kin, nor according to his dominion which he ruled. For his kingdom shall be plucked up, even for others beside those. 5, The king of the south shall be strong and one of his princes; he shall be strong above him and have a dominion; shall be a great dominion. 6

Now back to home church at Bee Bayou and Daniel Prophecy. The next week I was invited to the Brownsville Street church, in West Monroe. There was a revival going on. The evangelist was a woman that was at G.I. Temple's revival in Morgan City. She told me that she was filled with the Holy Ghost at Brother G. I. Temple's Morgan City revival. That is all God confirming the word of prophecy and all I spoke behind the pulpit on that Sunday. God confirmed His word!

BETHANY GOES TO REVIVALS WITH DAD

I was almost 18 years of age on July 17, 1968. The cotton crop was growing; it was almost harvest time. Dad had an invitation to preach revivals in South Louisiana. He made a trip to the Charenton Levy Church, pastored by Brother Jack Hitt. Brother Jack was retired worker at Brown and Root McDermont Oil Company. Our Temple family loved Brother Jack Hitt; he came to love our Temple people. He became a frequent and beloved minister holding revivals in our churches.

He carried his own small white enamel coffee pot. He made the strongest darkest coffee, only a Cajun could enjoy! I packed a few church clothes and got into Dad's truck and headed to Charenton, Franklin, Louisiana area. There was a huge old fashion wood house and next to it was the church which they built. We had good, anointed preaching and singing. The church was always full of people who needed prayers to be answered. Dad would encourage the people's faith to believe in God's miraculous healing power. As he rehearsed the two major miracles that took place in our own family, he always had me to stand as he told the congregation the whole testimony from beginning to end not leaving anything out. That is how a story should be told; do not leave anything out. Nowadays, people want you to get to the point. That is boring. You leave out the excitement of the miracle. It is sad today. The congregation was spellbound as they listened to details of the miracles that was like watching Jesus explaining, teaching, and taking his time, simply. They understood what he said, have faith, believe, and receive.

BETHANY IS MARRIED – YES, ANOTHER BEGINNING

The year was 1968, and I was 18 years of age. Here I am, the number is 8, again. Believe me, I did not plan it! My dad was holding revivals. I was 18 years of age and single. It was a big change for me, a transitioning time. I married a young man in December 1968. Dad's revivals were in South Louisiana. We lived in opposite directions, North Louisiana. To me, it was like it was on the other side of the world. Our family was a close loving Christian family. Everything we needed was right there on our 60-acre farm.

My husband was a commercial fisherman. He made good money. There were large expenses to keep his outboard motor operating.

He also had fishing nets that needed repairing. The weather was an issue that hindered his fishing success. This was not a problem at first when there was just the two of us.

I did not get out to meet people. That became a blessing for me, staying to myself. There is so much evil out there; God protected me. I was a virgin, a Christian, rooted in my godly teachings. As much as my husband was away from home, anything could have happened to me. My heavenly Father watched over me. I had a personal relationship with Jesus Christ from the beginning of my life. I did not know that I was chosen to work for Him until sometime later.

We did have financial problems from the beginning of our marriage. I knew nothing about finance. Dad and Mom had a great relationship. They discussed everything. My husband did not communicate with me. Good communication makes a good marriage. Talking together, learning about each other, and getting to know each other, bring husband and wife close together. That was a problem in my marriage. I was a strong, dedicated Christian; my husband was not. I could see that he did not get the Bible teachings that I did. I was concerned, but too late! Our marriage was a struggle from the beginning. Marriage is not about the bed. It is about working, doing things together and talking. That's how I was raised. Our family prayed together, grew together, learned, and yes, we stayed together.

Our marriage started on a dangerous rocky road. I was alone most of the time; I was lonely. This did not improve, until I began to have my children. I was no longer lonely. I had a different problem. My husband did not bring home enough money to meet our needs. We were no longer on the farm with my parents helping us.

BETHANY'S FINANCIAL TROUBLES AND STRUGGLES

We started having financial problems early in our marriage. My dad passed away two months after our wedding. Dad, Mom, and two carloads of family showed up at our house for the weekend. I was so excited. I did not have much food in the house because there were only two of us. I was self-conscience about not having extra food to prepare for the family. We always had plenty of food back on the farm.

Dad was getting Social Security payments at the time and brought me some money. I went to the grocery store and bought food with the money Dad gave to me. See how God came through, just in time?? He always does; He never fails His children! He makes a way when there seems to be no way. He is GOD!

This was the last visit that I saw Dad alive. The last thing I heard my dad say as he prayed, bowing to the floor, he asked God's blessings on me. He said if we never meet again on this side of heaven, he wanted to see me on the other shore. That was the last time I saw Dad. He passed and went to Heaven one day before his 62nd birthday, February 11, 1969. I thank God for that timely visit which was a blessing to me. When I received the news that Dad had passed, a good friend who lived next door, drove me to meet my nephew, Roger, who took me to Mother's. My husband was out on the water fishing. When he came home from fishing, he moved our household to Rayville, Louisiana. As time went on, we moved back and forth from Rayville to Venice.

BETHANY "TEMPLE OF GOD"

My family grew as God blessed us with four children. Our children were from 13 months and two years apart. It was difficult to get Food Stamps at that time. My fisherman husband had very little extra money for our household. After his paying for his equipment repairs, and paying bills, there was little money left for groceries. Every fishing receipt from income and expenses had to be reported to qualify for food stamps. I did not drive nor have access to a car at that time. This is like the old saying, "between a rock and a hard place." We lived in a mobile home park. Our landlord's granddaughter, Angel, tried to help us with this problem.

We did not go to church regularly. My husband took us to church on Sundays when he wasn't working. If I had been bolder, we could have got assistance from the church. This is one reason why we moved back and forth from Venice to Rayville. That was our life until the Lord heard my cries. We cannot keep our mouths shut with God. We must cry out to God and get His attention.

God began to bless my family and me. A lady from our church was the Head Custodian Supervisor at the Boothville Venice school. She called asking me if I would be interested in a job as Custodian at the school. I was excited and praised God as His blessings continued. We moved from the mobile home park to our own home. The Lord blessed me with a car, which my brother, Boyce, sold to me. I eventually sold it and bought better cars until I bought my first new car! My Father loves me. I love my Father God with all my heart, mind, body, soul, and spirit. I love my neighbor as myself. You cannot lose with God on your side. You will win, if in His love you abide. His door is always open if you just step inside. You can't lose with God on your side.

BETHANY'S THREE BLOODY MISCARRIAGES

I went through three bloody miscarriages. I had no family to help me. My first one was after a confrontation with my husband. I was frustrated and tired of the situation I was in. I was in the flesh, not strong in the Holy Spirit to keep me calm. I reacted and ran out the back door of our mobile home. I fell to the ground, which caused the miscarriage. I was not far along in my pregnancy. I called out through my troubled spirit, asking for God's help. I grew in faith and obedience to God. I had to grasp onto God for myself. I used to rely on the family's prayers. I grew stronger in God. I previously depended on Dad's prayers. Dad passed so I depended on my oldest brother's prayers. Ten years later he passed. Satan seemed to attack me stronger and more often.

The children and I went to Sparta, Tennessee, with our pastor and his family. I started bleeding during the trip. As time went on, I went to the bathroom often. I saw a blob in the toilet that I thought might have been the fetus. When we returned from our trip, we went to Rayville. During the Sunday church service, I was bleeding heavily. When the service was dismissed, I stood up and the bottom fell out. There was so much blood and chunks of tissue on the floor. The preacher and others came to me, crying out to the Lord for my healing. I will never forget that the preacher, began repeating a scripture in the Old Testament. "When I passed by you, I saw you polluted in your blood. I say, when you were polluted in your blood, to live. I said, when you were polluted in your blood, to live." The preacher told me to continue repeating those words, and I did. I went up the road to my sister's home and laid down in her bedroom. I was made whole that hour! I praised God!

Another time, just myself and small children were home alone. My husband was somewhere down the road, probably at the fish dock. I was bleeding all day. As the day grew late, my blood had covered the walls and floor in the bedroom. I had no telephone at that time. I do not know who let the neighbor know, but someone went down the road to the fish dock. A friend who lived closer to the dock got my husband, who called my mom in Rayville. That friend drove me the New Orleans Charity Hospital. The trip took longer than a hour to arrive at the hospital. I was taken directly to the examination room. The doctor took me to surgery to perform a DNC on me. The procedure aborted the fetus and cleaned everything up. The doctor said if I had not arrived when I did, I would have bled to death because I had lost so much blood. When I was discharged, Mom and those who brought her to my house had cleaned up all the blood. She loaded the children and me into car and took us to Rayville. Home Sweet Home, family!! God is the one we can depend on. To God be all glory!!!

BETHANY'S FIVE BLESSED CHILDREN

At Dad's funeral, my body was weak, and I fainted. I thought this was from seeing Dad in the casket. A few days later, I realized I was pregnant with my first child, Lawrence Dion. We moved from my parent's home in Rayville to Serepta, Louisiana. My husband found work in Homer, manufacturing mobile homes.

My sister had a daughter and was expecting her second child. Bro. Rayford pastored the church nearby that we attended. A camp meeting was in progress. Diane, Vincent, and I attended the services. An elderly man from Arkansas brought forth the message. He began giving out the Word of Knowledge and Prophecy. He walked down the aisle toward Diane and me. He stopped beside Diane and said that God was giving her the desire of her heart. Diane wanted a son. The preacher told her that her son would preach for the Lord during the end times. Then he said to me that the Holy Spirit said you will have a son who will be an end-time preacher. He will preach the messages for that time. My sister and I claim these prophecies for our sons.

LAWRENCE DION SMITH

My son was born November 4, 1969, at Springhill Hospital in Springhill, Louisiana. Lawrence Dion was born with lots of black hair and a patch of blond on the back. Mom had come to visit Diane and me for the birth of our babies. I had complications while giving birth; my body got very cold as I was near death. Mom was praying. She saw someone in the doorway dressed in white. She arose from her chair and went to the door to see who was there. The person had disappeared, Mom said. She looked down the hall for a while, but no one was there. Mom realized that it must have been an angel from the Lord, assuring her that all was well. Dion and I were discharged from the hospital healthy. His first few words were Mama, Daddy, and Look!

Dion grew up in Venice, Louisiana. His first job was at the IGA Super Market at the age of 15. I had to sign permission because he was underage. He has been working ever since. His last year of school, I bought him a car. Dion graduated at the top of his class; he was Salutatorian. He could have attended any university if I had known the procedure of applying for college entrance. My marriage was not in good shape at that time. I am sorry for what my children had gone through during their lives. My heart hurts not only for my children but also for other families who experienced pain and disappointments. It takes a godly father and mother being good examples to raise their children, according to the Word of God. I thank God that Dion did attend Louisiana Tech in Ruston, Louisiana. He is a very intelligent man, who worked many years at Fiber Bond, in

Minden, Louisiana. Later to currently, he works at Hanes, in Arcadia, Louisiana. He is not only a hard worker, but the father of my first grandchild. When I named Dion, I did not know it was a biblical name. I was reading in the book of Acts, where the name Dionysus appeared, Dion's name. He was one of Paul's converts at Athens. Paul was brought into the Aropagus at (g.v.) Athens to give account for his doctrine (34), "howbeit that a certain man clave unto him, and just believed his doctrine". Among them was Dionysus of Corinth. Dionysus was Avotary of Bacchus, the Areopagite. A woman named Damaris was with them, as well as others. Eusebius (hist. Ecclesiastes 3:40, 4:23).

Dion is chosen. Dionysus of Corinth, the Areopagite, was named the first Bishop of the Church of Athens. Suidas gives full account, according to the Dionysus who was born in Athens, studied in Egypt and became eminent for learning. While he was in Heliopolis and Egypt, seeing an eclipse of the sun, he exclaimed to a friend, "either the Deity is suffering, or sympathizing with someone who is suffering".

The eclipse took place at the death of Jesus Christ. Returning to Athens, he became an Areopagite; converted unto Paul and became a Bishop of Athens, by Paul. It is said that he suffered martyrdom at Athens. The name Dionysus became important in church history for certain writers. I am one of them!

Lawrence Dion married a beautiful young lady from Gibsland, Louisiana. They have one son, Nicholas Brandon Smith.

NICHOLAS BRANDON SMITH

Nick is my first-born grandchild, born May 25, 1993, in Lincoln General Hospital, Ruston, Louisiana. Like most first-time grandparents, I was proud of him. I wanted to show his pictures to someone, anyone! I had a picture of him in my work uniform pocket. The owner of the candy company was about to pass by me in the hallway. I stopped him as I took the picture out of my pocket and told him that this was my first grandchild. Nick was a big blue-eyed baby with light blond hair. The owner of the candy company stated that this baby looks he has already indulged in our delicious candy. We laughed about that!

My children usually received clothes for Christmas from me. I do not know what his other gifts from the rest of his family were. Nick had a large collection of dinosaurs. When I went to visit him, I would get on the floor with him and play. Occasionally, his Aunt Shanara would sit with us on the floor and play. We enjoyed our time and memories. Our families are precious! We are so busy when they are young that we don't take time to think about the most important things, which is togetherness. I admire dads and moms that raise their family to put God first in their lives; all things will fall in place.

When I attended school, we had safety meetings. These meetings were centered around being aware of strangers. It was not mentioned to be aware of family members who could harm you. Our hope today, is for the leaders of our nation, churches, and homes to return to God. Let us be as wise as a serpent and harmless as a dove. Let us crush that serpent's head under our feet!

Nicholas went to spend time with Shanara and me when he was older. We went to the largest mall in Louisiana, The Baton Rouge Mall. They enjoyed playing games in the mall. I missed many opportunities to get pictures of treasured moments of my children and grandchildren because I didn't have a camera. The memories are vivid in my mind; I thank God for a sharp mind, and for the memories from the beginning of my young life. God is so good! Sadly, that many people have dementia and Alzheimer's diseases.

If I were a painter, I could paint my memories vividly. A healthy mind and healthy body are from God. God watches over His children. We cry out to God each day and night for our children and loved ones. Our hearts hurt for the pain and sorrow that they suffer, and we are not there to help them. We call your name to our Heavenly Father. He is the one who knows what your needs are. The Holy Spirit will get your attention and save you just in time.

I love you very much, Nicholas! I thank you for your generous donation for the printing and publishing of my books. I appreciate you, my big man!! I am so happy that God has blessed you to enjoy your grandfather, Pete. Your grandmother, Henri, is a blessed bold woman, as she raised your mother. Nick, I love them! My prayers are for God to bless you all throughout your lives.

SIDNEY LYNN – BORN JANUARY 7, 1971, IN DELHI HOSPITAL, DELHI, LA

Sid was born thirteen months after Dion's birth. It was snowing that day and my brother, Boyce, drove Mom and me to the hospital. We stopped at Dorothy Rae's and left Dion with her. Boyce slipped down in the snow but did not drop little Dion. Mom named our second baby "Sidney", her niece Arabella, had named her first son Sidney. I named him "Lynn" after my niece, Lynette, for he was born on her birthday. Sidney was Mom's first red-headed grandchild. Boyce and Dee's first child, Cynthia, born two weeks later with red hair! Mom was excited to have two beautiful red-headed grandchildren born the same month! Sid loved to hold my hair when he was near me.

At some time, Mom spoke a word of knowledge over Sidney. She said that he was called to preach the gospel. Sid was dedicated to the Lord. He wrote notes in his notebook during church services and camp meetings. He was anointed by the Holy Spirit, on fire for God.

In 2017, the Lord used Sid mightily. He worked on the church campgrounds, helping with anything that needed to be done. He is a "Jack of all trades"; he knows how to do almost any job needed. God has given Sidney talents with "hands on learning". He was an honor roll student in school. The Word of God, the Holy Bible, flowed through Sid's voice, as he ministered behind the pulpit. People were blessed, all of them knew that he was called to preach. The boldness of the Holy Spirit showed through him; he was confident as if he had ministered for years. Satan was upset; he did not want Sid to give his will over to God to be done on earth as it is in Heaven. Satan lost his hold on Sidney!

During the 2017 camp meeting, Satan's bubble burst. Prior to 2017, Satan had been getting a hold on the powerful anointed camp meetings. People began to praise men and gave them the glory. God is a jealous God. He will share His glory with no man! Those people did not realize that the Holy Spirit moved out of the church. Silly women came into the house of God with doctrines of men. The leaders could not discern their voices to the Holy Spirit. A grieving Holy Spirit took over the few real men and women of God. The leaders of the church did not repent and return to God. Pride of the flesh would not allow them to see their wrongs. Sidney was on fire for God. He witnessed and put into writing, in his notebook, the demonic activities that went on in God's house. The Word of God that Sid spoke confirmed what the woman of God had spoken to the church regarding the same matter. The leader and the church people provoked God to anger with the abominations that went on in His House and on His property. God was no longer welcome in His own House.

Sidney was ridiculed for putting into writing the evil things that had happened in the church. Ezekiel 8, states that God sent for the men of the city with destroying weapons in their hands to slay all young and old, all who turned their backs on Him. They did not repent; it was a great slaughter. Every tongue that came against Sid and against the Word of God, have suffered because of their own doings.

I know that Grandma, Margaret Florene Wilson Temple

would be proud of Sid for speaking the truth, the Holy Bible. She used to say, "If the shoe fits, wear it." Let every man be a liar but God's Word, the Holy Bible is true. The evil ones were put to shame. They have a mark on them until they repent. When they repent, God will forgive and save them. God doesn't want anyone to perish. God's breath is within us; He made us living souls.

Sid ran this Gospel Race! There is no time to stop; there is no time to slack up. Time is running out! God is depending on His chosen few to finish whatever the cost may be. Remember all the suffering our Lord has gone through. Put the whole armor of God on; whatever weapons he comes against you with will not prosper. It will be like a boomerang; it will come back on him and bring him down.

With all the sevens in Sidney's name and events in his life, seven is God's signature number, meaning complete, finished. God chose him to work for Him. Sidney means cheerful, eager to live; Lynn means courageous.

SIDNEY LYNN'S MIRACLE

I did not realize that Sid was 48 years old and never had a driver's license. I had aged and needed Sid to drive me wherever I needed to go. I did not know that Sid had no identification. A lady had called me, saying that Sid was in Texas working for an oil rig drilling company. I told her that Sidney was at home and had not been anywhere working; this problem was cleared up. Sid received his identification card and papers from the one who had them.

Sidney attended drivers' education classes and passed the exam. He went to the Department of Motor Vehicles to get his license. There was a block on it. He would have to pay to clear the block.

I went to the Sheriff's office, introduced myself, and told him why I was there. He immediately made calls and found some information about the person who was using Sid's identity. He was busy and turned this case over to an investigator. He asked Sid several questions. He asked if the person who had Sid's ID was ever declared deceased. I had heard that his widow had declared him dead so her children could get Social Security from their dad. See God's timing on this situation? The investigator told Sid to go back to DMV to get his license. That's what we did. Sid was reluctant to return to DMV because he had been denied and didn't know that something had changed regarding this issue. He came out grinning, looking at his first driver's license at the age of 48! I love you, Sidney Lynn, my middle boy, who loved to hold my hair.

RICHARD SCOTT SMITH, BORN SEPTEMBER 13, 2005

Richard is the oldest child of my daughter, Shanara Angelle Smith. He is the grandson that I enjoyed raising in my older age. Sidney Lynn is his Popa; he is more like a dad than a Popa. Richard has enjoyed being loved and protected by Nanny and Popa. He grew up praising and loving God. When Richard was two years old, he wanted to go up on the platform where he saw the preachers ministering. I carried his mom's karaoke microphone to church in his diaper bag. We would get to church early before the people got there. He would get his microphone and climb up on the platform, ready to preach. As Popa and I was watching him, my sister, Dorothy Rae, came in. Richard was pacing from one end of the platform, screaming, and jabbering as if he was preaching. The only word that I could understand was 'donkey'. I would say, "Yes, brother; that donkey carried Jesus to Jerusalem." Dorothy said, "Brother Richard, that is powerful preaching, but I would like to understand the words." We have pictures of Richard 'preaching'.

A visiting preacher brought his demonstration replica of the Tabernacle. This was the Priest's ritual in preparing for God's sacrifice. Richard was listening very carefully to everything that the minister said. The scene was the lamb sacrifice with fake blood on his neck as if he was killed for the sacrifice. Richard was still two years old; he approached the lamb and put his little arms around the lamb's neck. It seemed that he understood the demonstration. We also have pictures of Richard with the Tabernacle exhibits.

BETHANY "TEMPLE OF GOD"

We had gone to another church, listening to the preacher's sermon about coming back to the Lord. Richard was standing in the pew beside me, stiffened his little legs with his little arms stretched out, his finger pointing to the minister; he yelled, "Put it back!" I don't know what other people in the congregation thought. I do know that Richard had heard many times, "Put it back", when he would be reaching for something that he was not allowed to have. God forgive me; I got the giggles. I managed to keep them to myself. Occasionally the giggles try to come back. Children are naturally funny with their sudden outburst of whatever comes to their minds. You have got to love them!

At our church one Sunday morning, people came in whom Richard had never noticed. He had watched a Sesame Street Movie which had an evil man character, who had taken Elmo's blanket. At this church service, Richard was standing next to me as he stiffened with excitement, upset with fear, and pointed to a man on the back pew and yelled, "There's that mean old Huxley"! It was a man who looked like the villain in the movie who took Elmo's blanket.

At home, he did like most children, pulling out pots and pans and sitting in them. Sitting in his walker in front of the TV, he watched commercials like 'People PC'. We have snapshots of Richard watching this. As he grew older, he would watch children sit on the floor and how they stood back up without holding on to something. It was not long before Richard could do the same. It was fun watching him as he made his first baby steps. He was a smart child as he paid attention to what he saw and heard and retained it. He was amazing! I was busy while my children were growing up and did not notice little things as they were learning. Being at home with Richard was a privilege, hearing and watching him learn, do, and say the cutest things. He graduated with the highest honors in his high school class of May 18, 2023. He was granted scholarships to attend Louisiana Tech in Ruston, LA. He plans to major in Animal Science and be a veterinarian.

TONY CLAY SMITH, SR.

My third child, Tony Clay Smith, Sr., was born November 22, 1972, at Delhi Clinic, Delhi, Louisiana. I went into labor the day before Thanksgiving and discharged the day after. My brother, John William, was working for Sun Oil Company in Delhi. When he got off work that day, he went by the hospital and prayed for me to have a safe healthy delivery. The doctor had come into the delivery room to examine me. He said that it looks like all we are doing is wasting my time and your money. As soon as he left the room, my baby was coming. I called the nurse. She came into the delivery room, complaining because the doctor had just come in and left. He didn't think it was time for the baby to be born. She said that the baby was still not ready. Tony was born before the nurse had time to prepare for his delivery. Tony came and she was bragging that she had delivered the baby. It was Big Buddy's prayer that got little Tony ready, in a hurry, to enter this world. Thank you, Jesus!!

When Tony reached kindergarten age, we lived in Boothville, Louisiana. At the end of his kindergarten year, he had a part to learn and recite for the promotion to the first grade. He surprised me at how well he spoke in front of the people at the celebration. His speech was "To Kindergarten, I must go for my mama told me so. I just cried and said, I'd rather stay with you instead. Math began and I almost choked. You have to learn to count so you don't go broke. Now, I know that 1 + 1 is 2. Now, Mom, does that really surprise you?"

Tony is my child who was very close to his Uncle Big

Buddy. When we would go to Rayville to visit our family, Tony was the first to get out of the car. He would run across the gravel road and through the woods on the trail to Big Buddy's house. He followed every step that my brother took. Mom gave each grandchild one dollar; Big Buddy would load his car with all the children and drive them to the Bee Bayou store to spend their dollar. In those days, they could buy lots of candy with a dollar. They were such happy little fellows; Mom loved all of them!

Tony loved being outdoors. He started working when he was a preteen with a fisherman/trawler whose name was Mr. Knapp, from Monterey, Louisiana. He received lots of experience working with fishermen. Tony still goes fishing every chance he gets. Those fresh fried fish are some good eating! Most of Jesus' disciples were fishermen; He even taught them about fishing as well as teaching them how to be fishers of men. He taught and illustrated in parables, like catching fish and then comparing to spreading the Gospel to all people to bring them into the Kingdom of God.

TONY, A TEENAGER

Tony spent time in Florida, in the home of my niece, Lynette Smith Walters, and her family finishing his high school. He was close to his cousins, Gordy and Joshlin Walters. His car broke down on his way home from Florida. He called me and I was happy to be able to go and rescue him. Tony graduated from Arcadia High School while staying with his cousins, James Roy and Shane Antee.

After a time, my brother-in-law, Jimmie Wright, pastor and husband of my sister, Nancy, gave Tony a job. They built cabinets in homes and built churches and parsonages in Oklahoma. While living in Oklahoma, Tony went to welding school and soon was a certified welder. He knows struggles in life. If I were rich, I would divide my wealth with my children for them to enjoy. They would not need to look at prices on things, wishing that they could purchase them.

Tony married Ashley Smith of Choudrant, Louisiana. They had a small black and white puppy named Little Ashley. She lived many long, happy years with lots of love during her life. Tony and Ashley have something in common; their grandpas both are named, Henry Clay (Wilson) and Henry Clay (Smith). They have two sons: Tony Clay, Jr. and Colton Garrett. Later they adopted a daughter, Sadie Marie. Sadie blessed her parents with a granddaughter, Emily Ann Smith.

TONY CLAY'S AUTO ACCIDENT

In 1991, Tony and Sidney were in a serious accident. I had just got a job at a candy company in Ponchatoula, Louisiana and had not started the job at that time. The boys' accident happened the weekend that I was supposed to begin my job. I had to report to my supervisor regarding my children being involved in the accident. I was only given enough time to drive from Ponchatoula to Shreveport to check on my boys. Sidney was hurt but would not go to the hospital. Tony was admitted to LSU Hospital in Shreveport with a broken jaw which was wired shut. Tony's tongue was swollen and caught between his teeth when the doctor closed his mouth. I noticed his expression and tears flowing from his eyes. I called the nurse and told her that Tony's tongue was caught between his teeth. They got busy and released his tongue. I had to get back to my new job, as soon as possible. I thank God that His hands were on my two boys.

Tony was in another auto accident in 2000 in Greenville, Mississippi, where he was hospitalized. His friend, Bubba and his mother, from Gibsland, Louisiana, happened to be in that area when the accident happened. Bubba took Tony's vehicle back to Gibsland. I stayed with Tony until he was released from the hospital. I took him with me to Greenville, Texas, where my sister lived. Her husband was pastor of the Church of God, in Greenville, Texas. I stayed a couple of days and left Tony there and I went back to work in Ponchatoula. Nancy and Tony were very close; he had stayed with them for a period.

Was this another coincidence – Greenville, MS, and

Greenville, TX? No, there is no accident, no incident, and no coincident with God! Wow! God is awesome!! Both Tony and Ashley's sons are pro-baseball players for the state of Lousiana. Tony, Jr. plans to major in Agriculture and Forestry at Louisiana Tech in Ruston and hopes to become a Game Warden. Colton plans to attend college with a baseball scholarship.

TONY CLAY SMITH, JR.

T. J. is the first child of Tony and Ashley Smith. He was born March 3, 2006, in Lincoln General Hospital in Ruston, Louisiana. He is six feet + tall! He is a baseball three times Louisiana Champion. He is a handsome young man. Our Temple and Smith families are proud of him. He will graduate from High School in school year 2023-2024. He plans to attend Louisiana Tech University and major in Agriculture and Forestry. He wants to be a Game Warden. He works on a nearby farm raising thoroughbred prize horses. T.J. has two horses, their names are Chevelle and Penny; they are Champion horses. T.J. attends rodeos every chance he gets.

Several years ago, Tony, Sr. took a picture of T.J. standing beside Laney Wilson, a singer/actress. A few years later, they realized that Laney is his cousin! My mom, Margaret Florene Wilson Temple, is sister to Laney's great-grandfather, Jesse Richard Wilson. Margaret Florene Wilson Temple is T.J.'s great-grandmother. This is not from Ancestry. Com. It's from the horse's mouth, me, Bethany Joyce Temple.

T.J. has several laying hens; one is sitting on eggs to hatch babies, and one rooster. T.J. grows a garden that produces several different vegetables which he has planted.

COLTON GARRETT SMITH

Colton is the second child of Tony and Ashley Smith. He was born July 17, 2007. Colton's birthday numbers are God's perfect numbers, meaning complete. He was born on my birthday, 7,17,1950, meaning complete and Pentecost. Colton drives his grandma, Nancy, to church on Sunday mornings. Colton bought a beautiful black wavy long-haired cattle puppy; her name is Dixie. He trains Dixie to herd cattle. He is also a Louisiana Champion Baseball player. He, as well as his brother, is tall at 6 feet +, handsome young man. His Grandma Bethany prays for their protection and game successes. Recently, both boys had baseball related injuries. I called out to Jesus; they were miraculously healed. I give praise to God!

SADIE MARIE SMITH

Tony and Ashley desired a baby girl. After several years, they hoped a baby girl would be available for adoption. Someone heard of an older little girl who was available for adoption. She wasn't what they wanted but they visited the little girl. Ashley became attached to her. After several visits to the orphanage, signing papers, and going before the judge, they adopted this little 8-year-old girl. Ashley thought she could mold this little girl to be a model child. Sometime later, Ashley and Tony were told of their new daughter's abusive lifestyle. The older she became, were trying times in their household. She was very verbal refusing to obey her parents and had problems in school. Her mom and dad took her to counseling, but she did not improve. When she was a preteen, she moved in with her uncle and aunt for a few years. She began dating and got pregnant. Sadie never went back home to live. She was 18 years of age on November 14, 2022. In December 2022, someone called Ashley saying that Sadie was in the hospital giving birth to a baby. Ashley went to the hospital after work. After the baby's birth and Sadie was discharged, Ashley took Sadie and the baby home with her. Sadie stayed about two months and spent lots of time on the phone talking with boyfriends. Sadie eventually moved, so Ashley's family helped with babysitting. Tony and Ashley took the responsibilities as Pawpaw and Meme. God turned this situation around for their blessing and now they are "Dad" and "Mom". God gave them their hearts desire! God does not necessarily come when we want him to, but He's always right on time. Remember God's words, to everything there is a time and a season for every purpose under the Heaven.

EMILY ANN SMITH

Emily Ann Smith is Tony and Ashley Smith's official new addition to their family! She was born December 20, 2022. She fits in our Temple family very well, with her beautiful red hair. Emily Ann, welcome to our Smith/Temple family! You are a blessing from God! The angels must have brought you to the Tony, Ashley, T.J., and Colton home. Thank you, Lord, for your blessings on us. Emily had been taken to the doctor on Friday afternoon. Her conditioned worsened; she was rushed to ER on Friday night, April 21, 2023 because she was vomiting, having trouble breathing and limp from lack of oxygen. After a thorough examination, the doctor determined that she had a severe sinus infection. I texted my prayer partner on Saturday morning at 1:00 A.M. Tony, Ashley, and Emily got back home at 7:00 A.M. It was a long tiring day. God gave little Emily a miracle! Through faith and works, taking Emily to the doctor, God gets all the glory and praise!

AMY YVETTE SMITH RIOS

Amy was born February 7, 1975. WOW!! Finally, my first daughter. Would you believe that I had her name picked out before my first boy was born? After three boys, I was ready to name her something else. The boys were now used to hearing Amy Yvette. They figured that her name had to be named Amy Yvette. So, it is! My mom had bright red hair; Amy is Mom's first red headed grandchild, who has three red headed grandchildren. All three of the children belong to Amy's oldest daughter. Amy is my first and only child to be born at E.A. Conway Hospital. Amy was a very intelligent child; she was an honor student all through school. She has God's blessed numbers in her birthday, the sevens. Her kindergarten teacher told the class to write on paper their favorite foods. Amy wrote chips, chips, chips!

Amy had issues with passing out/fainting. She would have dreams of angels pulling her into Heaven. I was concerned that she might be going to Heaven soon. She also said that angels were also trying to pull her dad into Heaven, but he would not go.

I called Mom at her home in Rayville; we lived in Venice, Louisiana. I told Mom about Amy's sickness and dreams. Mom began speaking in the Holy Ghost; then her gift of interpretations was spoken. The words of knowledge and wisdom were spoken, also. The word of God came to me that I needed to get the children in church and pay tithes. Mom did not know that I wasn't going to church nor paying tithes. The Holy Spirit spoke that through her. I obeyed God; went to church and paid my tithes. I met a woman in the church who asked me if I would be interested in a job at the Boothville school. She was the supervisor of the House Keeping Department. I said what better job could a person have than working at the same school where my children attended! I love my children that the Lord blessed me with, so much. I was no longer lonely! Soon, we had enough money to buy groceries and go to New Orleans shopping center. The children enjoyed playing on the game machines.

When I went to work at the school, my last child started to school. The Lord blessed me that I could purchase a car. Now, we could go to church when the children's dad was away working. We were blessed to be able to purchase our own home and property. God is so good and blesses those who serve him. These blessings came to us through obedience to the voice of God spoken by my mother through her home phone from miles away. My four children were well behaved. I didn't leave them at home when grocery shopping, etc. They pushed the shopping cart helping put groceries in and did not run around the stores.

MOSES IAN RIOS

Moses is Amy's first child born on July 20, 1994, in Houston, Texas. He was born with Autism/Asperger's disease. He is a very intelligent young man and a 'technical genius'. Moses is very verbal; he gets loud, provoking, and violent at times. I believe his outbursts are from growing up in a home of verbal abuse.

Moses likes to grocery shop, selecting his own foods. He walks to the corner quick stop with his mom to buy pizzas. One of his favorite foods is Nacho Bell Grande.

I remember when he was a small child, he loved his 'sit and spin' toy. He enjoyed things that spin around. He would push a chair close to the washing machine, smile, and giggle when he saw the clothes spinning so fast. He loved to watch the ceiling fan turning. These spinning and turning things fascinated Moses. I was amazed and excited when I learned that Moses had gone to the DMV and got his driver's license. WOW! My Moses made a big accomplishment! He is no longer a little boy; Moses has become a man. Moses was always interested in the weather reports, and we could depend on his report. At Camp meetings, he would give Sis. Barbara and other church folks, the weather reports. Each day, they would ask him what's the weather report today, Moses?

CHEYENNE NILDA RIOS STEVENS

Amy's second child, Cheyenne, was born on November 8, 1995, in Houston, Harris County, Texas. I remember that Amy would ask me to watch Cheyenne while she and her husband went out to eat, etc. Since they lived in Texas, Cheyenne did not know me because we didn't see each other often. I was in Gibsland visiting Dion and Nick during that time. They were living across the street across the street from the home that they bought later. Cheyenne ran across the yard, like lightning. To be so young, little Cheyenne was hard catch up with. I was afraid that she would reach the street before I could stop her. Cheyenne could have won a race against the best runner, as fast as her little legs were moving!

Amy and her children lived at Dion's front apartment in Gibsland, Louisiana, for a period. Nick's friend John was visiting him during the time that Cheyenne lived there. John and Cheyenne fell in love and married later. After they married, they moved to Highway 80, Minden, Louisiana. Their first child, Haley Rayne Stevens, with beautiful red hair was born on March 8, 2012, in Minden. Eventually, they moved to Oklahoma. A few years later, their second child, Aaren Parker Stevens, was born on June 13, 2016, in Bartlesville, Osage, Oklahoma. He was a handsome red haired baby boy! A couple of years later, Cheyenne gave birth to her third child, Avacyn Jane Stevens, born on August 23, 2018, in Bartlesville, Osage, Oklahoma. Currently, I have not met the last two great-grandchildren. Jonathan Stevens' grandmother and Ashley Smith's grandfather are brother and sister.

ANGEL JOYCE RIOS

Angel Joyce is Amy's third child, born on November 11, 2000, in Rayville, Richland, Louisiana. She was a beautiful baby and is a lovely adult! After she graduated from high school in Oklahoma, she enlisted in the National Guard. She is an intelligent young woman. She has remained close to her younger brother, Dexter. When Dexter graduated from Gibsland high school, in 2022, Angel called to congratulate him. She wanted to take him to Oklahoma with her to live there. I felt it was best for Dexter to remain at home. He was stable and his mom, Amy, lived next door.

I love Angel. My heart hurts for her; she has gone through much abuse and disappointments through her life. She, like many children today, does not know what real love is. All of God's people should wake up and show God's true love to all children. Satan is always lurking around with his lying, seducing, lustful spirit to lure them into hell. Our family must cry out to God, that he will hear our pleas for our children to accept Jesus Christ as their Savior. The love of Jesus is what heals the hurts of their tender hearts. Angel and I have always been close, from her birth to today. God save our children!!

XAVIER ODAMUS DEXTER RIOS

Dexter is Amy's fourth and last child was born on November 13, 2001, in Rayville, Richland, Louisiana. He was a beautiful little baby! He was born with Autism/Asperger's disease. Dexter is an amazing young man. He graduated from Gibsland high school in May 2022.

Some people do not understand Autistic children. Many are abused by school officials, and people in general. Dexter was a perfect example of a child mistreated in his school. He was accused of deliberate misbehavior in the classroom. When he was pressured, he would shut down, not speak, nor do his schoolwork. This was a symptom of Autism. My heart was broken for my grandchild!

There was a field trip planned for Dexter's class. The trip was going to tour our Louisiana State Capitol in Baton Rouge. He was so happy, so excited about going on this trip!! I signed the authorization forms, giving my permission for him to go to Baton Rouge with his class and sent the money needed for the trip. His form and money were sent home saying that he was denied traveling with the class on the trip. They were prejudice regarding my autistic grandchild. He was so sad; his heart was broken! My heart does hurt and is broken because my little man does not understand why he could not to go. I trust God; He sees everything.

SHANARA ANGELLE SMITH

Shanara is my fifth and last child, born on March 19, 1987, in Gretna, Jefferson, Louisiana. She was born twelve years after Amy. You know before I write this that she is a spoiled child.

I was working the whole time that I was carrying her. Most people did not know that I was pregnant until the end. I had good insurance with the Plaquemine Parish school system. I was blessed with many things that I would not have had otherwise. I thank God, most of all, that His word is true in blessing me. We need to be obedient children and follow him.

Shanara's delivery date came; we were blessed with a new hospital. We were among the first few to enjoy this new facility. I thank God for it. I did not deserve such royal treatment. Our Jesus Christ, our King was born in a lowly stable in a bed of hay. There is a message in His simple lowly birth. He came from Heaven to Earth to be an example for His followers to live by. With this child, I was given an epidural injection before giving birth to her. I had to press the pillow to my stomach as I sat on the side of the bed. I could not move while they were injecting the medicine in my back. This injection was used to numb my lower back down to my feet, so I would not experience pain. I was not drowsy or sleepy but I heard someone say that she must be tired; she's going to sleep. I spoke up right away and said I am not sleepy; it feels like the numbing is rising higher than it needs to. They immediately called the anesthesiologist into my room; he worked fast to adjust the medicine. Another exciting experience was when it was time for delivery. The doctor came in and examined me. Shanara had her arm over her head, stopping the delivery. The doctor let me know that if she didn't put her arm down soon, I would need to have a cesarean section birth. Believe me, I did not want to go through that; I wanted to give birth naturally. I began to pray; God began to intervene. It was just a matter of time, that Shanara moved her arm down and the nurse rolled me into the delivery room. She was born a healthy little girl. God always delivers on time!! When I was discharged from the hospital, I was given a huge complimentary basket to take home.

My marriage ended about two years later and we moved to Ponchatoula, Tangipahoa, Louisiana. My brother-in-law got me a job with the insurance company that he worked for. My sister kept Shanara a lot while I worked. As I was on my sales collection route, in the local area, there was a little church. I saw a van just like mine and turned into the church driveway. The pastor and his wife, Bro. and Sis, Rattler, immediately welcomed me. Their church had prayer meetings, during the noontime, with those who were dedicated to see souls saved. They were born again, Holy Ghost filled, servants of God.

Shanara and I were invited to their beautiful home. They fell in love with Shanara at first sight. They wanted to babysit her while I worked. They had two older daughters and a son who was Shanara's age. She would ride to church and to revival services with them. On their way back home from a church service, Shanara was tired and kept saying to them that she was going to conk out. They told her to conk out!

She attended Ponchatoula schools. She received her

diploma through the GED program. She was employed by the candy company where I worked. She started dating a young young man who was in the Air Force National Guard. One morning while sitting in the candy company break room, Shanara was leaning against my arm. As I looked down at her face, she looked mysterious. A thought came to my mind, as I said to her, "Are we on the Jerry Springer Show?" She said, "Yes." That is how and when I found out my daughter was pregnant. She called the young man to let him know about the baby. He did not want to take responsibility as being a dad. He never has been a part of Richard's life. Our Temple people have a lot of love from our Father and that is lots of love for our little Richard Scott Smith, nick named 'Skittles'.

All of Shanara's prenatal doctor appointments were in the next town, Hammond, Louisiana. She was scheduled to delivery at North Oaks Hospital. Hurricane Katrina arrived; we had to move to Northwest Louisiana to my son's home in Gibsland.

When we arrived there, we did not know that the storm had made a turn from the course it was going, to the New Orleans area, which is where we lived. We had to make an appointment for Shanara at Lincoln General Hospital, Lincoln Parish, to continue her prenatal care. They did a sonagram showing a healthy baby boy. September 13, 2005, Richard Scott was born! When he was born, the umbilical cord was wrapped around his neck. I watched as the doctor carefully positioned the baby, then moved her hand between the cord and his neck and carefully moved the cord over his head. It was beautiful to watch his life beginning spared. Thank you, Jesus, for our new baby, Richard; he is a sweetheart.

In my son's house, I was Nanny to Richard; he called his uncle Dion, DooDoo and he called his uncle Sidney, Poppa. Dion and Sidney are Shanara's brothers.

Richard was born with a lazy eye, meaning that his eyelid only opened halfway. He had to wait until he was two years old to have surgery to correct it. The surgery was not dangerous; it was just sad to see the baby go through this. After he was released from the hospital, tears flowed from his mom's eyes. When we arrived home, she took him out of the car and felt what he had gone through.

After Richard was okay, Shanara was ready to move back to Ponchatoula and take him with her. I told her that she wasn't financially able to care for him, having no place to stay. She knew that it was best for Richard to stay with us. She signed a document giving us authority to send Richard to school and to handle his medical needs, etc.

Shanara left Richard with Dion, Sidney and me. He has been with me from his birth to this day. I feel like he is my son, instead of my grandson. He graduated May 18, 2023, from Gibsland Coleman High School, receiving scholarships to attend Louisiana Tech University in Ruston. Shanara now has three more children: Noah Alexander Autin, Raven Amelia Smith, and Luna Ashlyn Coates.

NOAH ALEXANDER AUTIN

Noah is Shanara's second child and son, born September 11, 2008, in Hammond, Louisiana in North Oaks Hospital. His dad is Howard Autin, of Hammond, Louisiana. Noah's number 9-11, meaning emergency, disaster, trouble. The number eight represents the eight people who were saved on Noah's Ark. Alexander means strong warrior. I was blessed to have Shanara and Noah in our home. She had moved back to Gibsland for a period. I have many pictures of Richard and Noah during the time they were together. Noah went to church with his brother, Richard, Poppa Sidney and Nanny Becky. Noah is currently living in South Carolina. He remembers what he has learned in church while attending church with us. He knows that God is our creator, our Heavenly Father, and Jesus Christ is God's son, our Savior. He knows God's Holy Spirit lives within us. I thank God for putting God's Word into Noah's heart. His favorite color is yellow. I love my grandchildren very much; each one is different, but they are the same in my heart, full of love. I pray that each one is saved before leaving this world. If we never meet again this side of Heaven, I want to meet you, Noah, on the other shore.

RAVEN AMELIA COATES

Raven is Shanara's third child and first daughter, born September 3, 2012, in Hammond, Louisiana. Her dad is Jesse Coates. Amy and I were blessed to be with Shanara when she gave birth to Raven Amelia. I had taken Dion's green truck for Shanara to drive taking care of her business. Raven looks like the Coates'. She is also the first grandchild and the first granddaughter of her Coates grandparents. They have spoiled this little girl. She moved with her mom and siblings to South Carolina, a couple of years ago.

Raven's favorite color is pink. Macaroni and cheese is her favorite food. She has no favorite animal. She has a favorite stuffed animal that's named, "Kitty". Her favorite game is Pin Up. She has no favorite movie.

Raven is very artistic. Her drawings are exceptional! She gave some of her art work to two of her aunts, her nanny Becky, and her grandmother Coates.

LUNA ASHLYN COATES

Luna is Shanara's fourth child and second daughter, born March 15, 2014, in North Oaks Hospital, Hammond, Louisiana. Her dad is Jesse Coates. Luna was born with black hair like her mother's. Her Coates family were wondering where her black hair came from. Shanara's hair was dark black when she was born. Her Smith people had black hair. Luna is my youngest grandchild. I have three great-grandchildren. Her favorite colors are pink and gray. Her favorite game is Roblox. Her favorite movie is Jungle Book. Her favorite food is pizza rolls. Kiki is her favorite stuffed animal. Her favorite animals are chickens.

BETHANY USED IN GIFTS AND INTERPRETATIONS

As I drew closer to God, He drew closer to me. I had gotten so low in the Spirit and sadness. I went into my bathroom in our mobile home on the property that the Lord had blessed us with. We were no longer renters! A Spirit of heaviness gripped me. At that time, I felt alone and lonely. It seemed that nothing was going right. Little did I know that God was beginning to turn things around in my personal life.

I picked up a razor blade from my bathroom sink cabinet. I had thoughts of cutting my wrist. I slid down the cabinet to the floor. Tears flowed down my face as I began crying out to God for help. That was the Holy Spirit interceding to God for me. Some do not understand that it takes cries from within our heart to get God's attention, not from our lips. God knows that I am His child; He knows the devil's tricks. Satan wanted to take my life so I would wake up in hell with him. The Lord ministered to me.

I began to talk to God. I first repented of my thoughts and weaknesses. I told the Lord that I had not served Him with my whole heart. I had not totally surrendered my will to Him. I told God, now, that I had given Him my all; I had given my will totally to Him, to be used as He chose. That was the turning point of my life. God began to use me in tongues and interpretations in our local church and to other churches that I visited and attended.

Sometimes, when the Lord used me in tongues and interpretations, the message would be the same scriptures that the minister preached. That was confirmation of the Word.

I grew in the Holy Spirit, gradually learning God's ways and not mine. The Holy Ghost was molding and making me in His likeness. I learned that I was different and could not and would not fit in with the crowd. I am a peculiar person, to show forth Jesus Christ in me and through me. The hardest thing I've had to learn is patience. I thought I had patience, but I found out that I did not. I told the Lord that I want to walk in His footsteps. That is when I realized that I did not have patience. Just like the followers, they would ask Jesus why he waited so long. They did not understand that when Jesus gets there, He is always on time. Jesus is the Healer, whenever He arrives. Jesus is the Resurrection and the Life. He is never late; He is always on time. A chosen man or woman must get that point to separate from fleshly desires to the desires of the Holy Spirit. He leads and guides us in His path. Now, do you want to tell me what I am supposed to do? I do not do my own will; I certainly will not do your will. This is the end of the matter. It is no longer I, Becky, but it is me, Bethany, in Jesus Christ, doing God's will, His plan, and His purpose. Revelations 2:17, "He that hath an ear, let him hear what the Spirit says to the churches. To him that overcomes, I will give to eat of the hidden manna, I will give him a white stone, and in the stone, a new name written, which no man knows, except he who receives it." My white stone has my new name, Bethany. I am eating hidden manna which is the Word of God. I'm an overcomer. It is no longer I, but Jesus Christ living in me, working, speaking through me as I obey His voice.

BETHANY'S PROPHECY GIVEN TO ME

I began to receive prophecies and words of knowledge after yielding my will to God's will. The enemy was determined to bring me down. When we yield our will to God, Satan trembles. It is not easy for him to overpower us. We overpower him and put him to flight. Greater is He, the Holy Spirit, that is within me, than he that is in the world (Satan). We have the power.

Bro. Foster was my pastor in Venice for a long time; he called me to the front of the church. He said, "Daughter of Zion, I see God using you. You are standing on a high mountain. There are jagged rocks all around; the enemy is hoping you will fall. I see your hair and your clothes blowing in the wind. Be encouraged, God has you in His hands."

My pastor at the New Orleans church on the Old Mason Strip Bar Street, said God was transitioning me. That was a difficult period in my personal life. I fasted and prayed constantly. I lost a lot of weight; the people I worked with the school knew part of what I was going through. I would hear the whispers pitying me for losing so much weight. Fasting and praying gave me lots of spiritual strength. People thought that I was grieving because of what I was experiencing in my personal life. God was building me up, preparing me for what I was about to have to deal with. It was the hardest time I had ever gone through my personal life and the longest time. God was my strength. This pastor referred to me as a messenger of God. A messenger gives out only the message that God gives him/her.

No more and no less! Tell it, then leave! Just like the angels of God speak only the message that God gives him to say.

MY SCHOOL JOB STOLEN

My marriage, family, and job were all in jeopardy. The Lord continued to use me in dreams and visions. These were clear words from God, what the enemy had planned against me. This is a dream that I had. "It all began as I was walking with the principal of the school. It was as if we were looking at houses and property. Suddenly, the principal moved with choler. He was very angry about something." I had just read in the Word of God about the enemy king moving with choler. I looked up the meaning of the word. It means vicious anger.

I understood later what the dream meant. That evil angry spirit actually came against me, a Christian, a child of God. We are in a spiritual warfare, evil against good. Satan will attack you for no reason. I was in the line of fire.

The principal was upset because a man from Virginia came to Louisiana and got the top job. The man had applied for the advertised position for the Plaquemine Parish School Board Superintendent. He had the credentials and was given the job. One can understand the vicious anger any local Louisiana person would experience expecting that job to be theirs. That is what happened in this situation. The 'enemy' schemed to have the new Superintendent fired.

My coworker's daughter had moved to the area. She was looking for her daughter a job; Mr. Principal obliged her. This is the perfect plan that he plotted. They did not know my God!

Lies went through the Principal to the School Board.

The principal wrote me up that I had quit my job. It was no longer a position. I received a dismissal letter stating that I was no longer employed. I called the superintendent and wrote letters regarding this matter. I told him that I did not know what was going on. I told him my story, the true story. I received a letter stating that he was looking into the matter for me. I found out that my friend's daughter was working in my department doing the job that I had done, which I was told no longer existed. I told him that if I was not needed, why was this woman doing my job in my department. The superintend told me that he would go through the legal process to find out what happened.

This is the summary of the whole matter, being obedient to the will of God.

To obey is better than to sacrifice. My friend's daughter wanted to work with her mother. Her husband's job had transferred him to our area at their request. She had talked to the principal about her daughter a job. The principal was upset with the superintendent because the superintendent was given the job that the principal thought he should have. The superintendent would be blamed for giving my job to someone else. This was the principal's plan, to cause the superintendent to lose his job. The plot turned on him. He was reprimanded for his wrongdoings in letting me go. God watches over His Word; His wonders He performs. My Heavenly Father watches over me.

BETHANY'S FIRST TIME STREET MINISTRY

I began to ask God's direction in what was next in my life. He showed me that I needed to witness to people about His love and salvation plan. I talked to my church friend, in Venice, Louisiana, about ministering on the streets. She did not have a vehicle; therefore, she walked wherever she needed to go. She was eager to be involved in the street ministry. I drove to her house and parked the car. We took our Bible from house to house, knocking on doors. We encountered many situations at these homes. We ministered the Holy Word and prayed for their needs to be met. The Lord blessed our ministry for putting His work first. While God was taking care of my business, I was doing His work. We continued about three weeks; then God answered my prayers. I received a very apologetic letter from the Plaquemine Parish Superintendent. A mistake had been made. I was compensated for a month that I lost, including interest on that month's salary. God gave back my pay plus interest that the 'enemy' stole from me.

My friend's daughter and family transferred to her husband's place of work. The principal's greed for the top job, the spirit of choler, vicious anger controlled him to do wrong to an innocent person, me, Bethany!! God saw all of it; there is nothing hidden from God.

BETHANY'S TROUBLED MARRIAGE

As time went on, my husband stayed around his fishing buddies more than usual. His buddies talked filthy and mistreated their families. They looked and lusted at pictures of women in adult books and magazines. Once I looked in my husband's wallet and saw folded advertisements to order sexual items. I would go with my husband to visit his fishermen's wives and families, being polite to them, talking about the Bible and Jesus. The evil spirits were stirred because I was in their territory speaking about Jesus. Sometimes when we would get in the vehicle to leave, there would be a page torn from their magazine on the seat of our vehicle.

Changes take place in a person's character and spirit when they keep company with ungodly people. "Birds of a feather, flock together." If you are a Christian, you will show yourself godly; if you're not, you will say and do as they do. The more frequently you associate with sinner friends, the corrupt thoughts can take control of your mind. Evil spirits move inside and manifest in and through you. My husband became angrier, and the evil spirits had him accusing me of the things that he was guilty of. The devil speaks with a forked tongue; he tries to speak the truth and lies at the same time. A Christian will not speak both; either they will be all truth, or all lies. One always knows the enemy when he tries to speak the truth. He is of his father, the devil, the father of all lies. He is a liar!

BETHANY'S MESSAGE OF LOVE

When Satan comes to bring you down, God always comes forth with His message of encouragement. When you love your God with all your heart, mind, body, soul, and spirit and love your neighbor as yourself, you have fulfilled the greatest commandment. God will put His arms of love around you. He will protect you from evil. Satan will try to harm you, but he will not succeed. I remember when I was expecting my last child, my husband was so angry that he threw the alarm clock down at me on our bed. The clock missed me and bounced to the floor! I am referring to evil spirits using someone, not the individual. Either a good spirit or an evil spirit will occupy our minds and bodies. If we are a child of God, His Holy Spirit dwells in us. We are not a child of God if we have not repented of our sins nor acknowledged Jesus as our Savior. We need the Holy Spirit inside of us to give us power to overcome evil. He will teach us, lead, and guide our path as we walk in His footsteps. We must follow Jesus' teachings, not a favorite teacher or preacher who give their beliefs, theories, and doctrines. Continue with Jesus and you will never fail. Call on Him, cry out to Him and he will hear you. He will answer you according to His plan and purpose in your life. This is what I learned throughout my life. I learned to lean on Jesus. He wants everyone to depend on Him for everything. Where Jesus leads me, I will follow Him all the way, every day.

BETHANY'S DIVORCE

As time continued, things nor my husband turned around for the better. The situation got worse not just for me, evil spread throughout our household. My children were affected. A friend and coworker talked with me one day on the job. She said that my child had told her that they were being touched and molested. The evil spirits became bold, aggressive, and unashamed, in my household. The friend had just bought a new mobile home and said that if we needed a place to stay that we could clean the old mobile home that was parked behind her new one and live in it. I told her that I needed to wait for the right time to move. "This was the straw that broke the camel's back", meaning that this has gone too far. One day I sat down on the sofa and said that we needed to talk. I told him that if things do not change, I would leave. He spoke up with a rough demonic commanding voice; I knew it was an evil spirit speaking through him. He said, "You cannot leave me. You've got to live with me until death do us part." I said, "I did marry you until death do us part, but in peace." He spoke up with a more satanic voice, saying, "There will be no peace!" I said, "yes, there is going to be peace for me." He stomped out of the house.

Remember, I had been fasting and praying, continually, it had become a daily part of my life. My pastor in New Orleans was still praying for and my transitioning during this troublesome time. The pastor did not give her advice as to what to do; the Holy Spirit lead me.

BETHANY'S BOYS MOVED TO RAYVILLE

The time had come for me to move down the road to my coworker's home. I took the two girls and our clothes; school was almost out for the summer. When he came home from a fishing trip, he was furious when he realized that I was gone. He went to where I was staying trying to persuade me to go back to him. I was safe there. If I had not used wisdom, and gone back with him, I probably would have experienced more abuse than before. But I stood my ground. After stalking me, I was never alone for him to able to force me to go with him. Again, the wisdom of God was my help. Summertime had come and school was out. The custodians had to remain at school to clean it to be ready for next year. I was busy cleaning the classrooms and bathrooms when he suddenly appeared without warning! I screamed and spoke aloud when he was trying to force himself on me. My head supervisor noticed his vehicle parked outside and called the police department. That was the last time that I had trouble with him. As soon as school was out, he had already moved the boys to Rayville. I hated for my boys to have to go with him. This is how things went down at that time. I did not know where the girls and I would end up. My friend, Sister Hilda, babysat the girls for me. My oldest daughter went to my brother-in-law, Vincent, and my sister, Diane's home and stayed with them. When school started, she went to school with her cousin.

I thank God for blessing my three boys to live with my Temple family. I know they went through hard times and struggles, like many children from broken homes. I have shed many tears for my boys. I was struggling to find where I fit in, as I was seeking God to show me, to direct my path. I did not dare follow my boys to Rayville. I'm sure that I would have gone to be with them; knowing that he was there, I would not have moved. If I had moved to Rayville, I would have been trapped in the situation that God delivered me from.

God is a jealous God. He was leading me, then. He is my number one husband. The Bible says that our maker is our husband. God has chosen me for a specific work in His kingdom. The things I experience are training for me. He wants me to be able to stand when the battles get rough. I will fight strong and proudly to defeat the enemy. The war will be over; there will be victory for you and me. God's hand has been on me from the beginning. God led me to places I moved to; He led me through things I went through. He used my mouth to speak His words of love, His words of salvation; I am anointed for battle.

BETHANY'S SHORT STAY IN NEW ORLEANS

I moved to New Orleans with my two girls; Sister Hilda was still my babysitter. I remained an employee at Boothville, Venice School. The drive to and from each day became tiring. My girls had to get up early to be dropped off at the babysitter, and then I had to travel on to work. I gave my two weeks' notice and filed for my retirement benefits. A New Orleans church lady and I split the cost of an apartment. One time, my part of the rent money was missing. We found out that her little boy went into my bedroom and took my money. He had gone to a nearby store and bought toys. That was easy to determine what happened to my part of the rent cost. This created a small conflict because I didn't have any money to pay my share. She did make her son return some of the items that were not opened. Another lady at the church offered me to stay at her house. I did not know this lady very well. My vehicle had all our belongings in it. We only had a few clothes inside her house. I had problems with her brother who lived there with her at their mother's home. My daughter and I slept with the lady of the house. I kept my purse close to me in the bedroom, but I had put my tithes hidden in my locked van. Her brother must have picked the lock. When I was ready to pay my titles, I could not find the money.

BETHANY MOVES TO LAPLACE

My school retirement finally came through. I moved from New Orleans to LaPlace. Now that I had money, I purchased a mobile home on the front lot of the trailer park. It was already set up to live in, furniture and everything. Owning my home, I only had to pay for space that the home was sitting on. I could finally move my belongings from the vehicle into my house. The space rent was $100.00 a month. I had deposited my retirement money in the bank. I was not a wasteful spender of my money. That was a blessing for me since I had low paying jobs. I had to work for money to keep coming in, so my retirement account would not be depleted. Besides the $100.00 monthly trailer space, I had to pay for utilities and gas for my vehicle to go to work. I ministered to people in the projects. Due to my low job income, I knew that I needed to move where I could find a higher paying job. My brother-in-law got me a job where he worked, in Ponchatoula, selling and collecting insurance. I did not get much business in LaPlace so I had to make a decision to move from there.

BETHANY'S MOVE TO PONCHATOULA

I had my mobile home moved from LaPlace to Ponchatoula. It cost a lump sum of my retirement money to move it. I could see God's hand in every relocation. I liked living in Ponchatoula. It's a small town like Rayville; the layout of the stores, the dry cleaners, hardware, clothes, and shoe stores are similar. We would walk down the sidewalks, sometimes stopping to visit. It had a warm friendly atmosphere. Nowadays, those areas are like a ghost town; the stores are all in a mall. At malls, you park and go inside in stores of crowded people with no personal conversations.

I witnessed too many people as I sold insurance and collected payments. I met a pastor and his wife in Ponchatoula when I stopped at their church. (They had a van identical to mine parked in their driveway.) I had passed the church, but a thought came to mind to turn around and go back. That's what I did. They were a blessing to me and my baby girl. I never was blessed with lots of money, but I was blessed moneywise in many other ways. Little is much when God is in it.

My baby was two years old when I met a man in Ponchatoula. She attended school there until Hurricane Katrina hit that area in 2005. We married in 1991. This man previously had insurance with the company that I worked for, but he let it lapse. He was a good provider for our home. One thing that I learned while working for the insurance company was to go to clients who previously had insurance but lost it and to reinstate it for them. I wasn't familiar with the area, nor am I a talker;

both prevented me from succeeding in the insurance business.

I applied for a job at a local candy company and was hired. The day I was supposed to begin my job, two of my boys were in an auto accident, referenced in Chapter 13, Bethany's Five Children. I enjoyed working at the candy company, being around people. One must be mature, wise, knowledgeable, spirit-filled, and disciplined to work with all types of people.

When the owner of the candy company retired, he gave his oldest son his position. They were good bosses. I can't say the same about the supervisors that the employees report to. I heard many employees complaining about being mistreated by the supervisors. I prayed and talked with God about this situation. This one thing that I will tell is something that bothered me was the time for raises. I overheard a couple of the supervisors talking down about the workers regarding their pay raises. I heard the workers saying that some had received one cent, some received two cents and some five cents. This was humiliating! The bosses were laughing at what they had done to these hard workers! The holy boldness rose up in me. I had the opportunity when they were alone to ask them why they gave them such a low raise and were still employed. If they did not deserve more money than a few cents, they should be fired. I could see that their expressions changed while speaking to them. Some of them professed to be Christians. They did not like me; they gave me a hard time from then on.

My Christian coworker lost her daughter-in-law and two grandchildren in a housefire. One of these bosses made remarks about her missing work for the funerals. It was only a short time later that one of these bosses lost his grandson. When we have mercy and compassion for others, God's mercy, and compassion flow through us. These are Christian characteristics. To our Heavenly Father, all of us are special and precious in His sight.

When I started my job, my boss said that she was a Christian; she was double-minded. She straddled the fence. A double-minded person is unstable in all their ways. Many are in the valley of decision. They try to be like their friends to fit in with the crowd. This is like trying to hold on to God, and to the world at the same. We cannot serve two masters; either we will hold on to one and hate the other.

This person gave me hard times with remarks about me personally. She made comments against me in the presence of employees who would laugh about things she was saying, for example, when I was reading the Bible on my lunch break. Someone had brought a Bible and left it at the guard desk. The guard on duty had handed the Bible to me. My boss told me that the Bible should be left at home on a shelf.

I worked the day shift. My supervisor would go in to relieve me in the afternoon. As soon she came in, she would give me more work than what was on my job description, expecting me to complete everything before I left for the day.

I tried befriending her from the time I was hired. It was a certain group of workers that she was trying to impress. This went on over a year.

At the beginning of my shift as I scanned my timecard, the people who were there were looking my way. I looked down the hallway thinking that they had seen someone behind me coming to work. They were looking at me! The guard or someone had asked me if I knew what had happened. I told them that I had not heard anything; I didn't have a clue what they were talking about. The guard informed me that my boss/supervisor had gotten killed in a car accident on her way home from work. The funeral was closed casket because she was decapitated. This was sad and chilling what Satan did to this poor soul! The obituary showed her positions in her church as being a church worker. What about being a worker in the Kingdom of Heaven? It is so sad! Even though I was mistreated by this person, my heart was more than sad regarding the outcome of this tragedy.

The Lord gave me favor with the owner of the candy company where I was employed. I saw open visions while working there. In one of the visions, as I was cleaning the restroom of the breakroom, the umbilical cord of the owner's pregnant wife burst which spewed blood onto me. My eyes blinked as if the blood actually splattered on me.

The next day, the owner did not show up for work. He was at the hospital with his pregnant wife. She was getting emergency surgery to save the baby. When he returned to work, he started talking to me as if he had already told me what happened to his wife. It is God who knows all things; He is the one who told me this secret.

A young preacher who worked at the candy company took gospel tracts to distribute to the people. Some people made remarks about him for bringing the tracts to the job. At some point, he gave them to me. I would ask people if they would like to read them; so, I put some on the table. People had a choice to take them or leave them. No one was harassed to take any; the evil ones caused trouble. I was told not to leave any of the tracts on the tables, again. A couple of the Christian ladies said that we could leave some of them in the ladies' restroom.

The female guard and supervisor over the temporary employees, reported us to the top management and to the owner of the plant, complaining about us leaving Christian literature in the restroom. We were taken to a meeting; the accusers were reprimanded concerning the issue.

The company manager was demoted to the plant supervisor because the plant manager became ill and could no longer do his job. An advertisement for the candy company plant manager position was posted. A man from Tennessee applied for the job and was hired. He was a Christian man; the other supervisors gave him a cold shoulder. They would not cooperate with him. Every chance that I had I would encourage him. God had given me an open vision at that time. I saw this man come into work late; his face was flushed red. I wasn't given the whole picture in the vision. I did tell him what I saw. Sure enough after that, he came to work and his face was blood red. He told me that his car had run off the road and turned upside down. After trying to work with these evil people, he gave his notice to leave the company. When I found out that he was leaving, I approached him and let him know that I was sorry to see him go. I told him that I would tell him something that my dad told me the last time I saw him, that if I never see him again this side of heaven, I want to see him on the other side. This man told me that he would see me again. All praise to God our Father, creation of all!

The head bosses over the plant where candy was made and packaged were difficult to work for. They were rude to the workers. It was worse when they made it an open show in front of other employees. When those types of bosses disrespect you, they show their true colors. I told the owner about how these supervisors behaved. They should be good examples for their employees. The owner told me to not be concerned about their actions and that I have a job there as long as I want. Their ugliness was increasing; I know they had in mind for me to quit my job. My Heavenly Father watches over me.

As I passed by one of the men one day, he asked me who told me that I could talk about Jesus and the Bible. I told him that Jesus said for us to spread the gospel of His Kingdom. I asked him who gave him the right to say such things that he says. He shut up and went back to his job.

I try to move as the Holy Spirit leads and guides me; I want to walk in Jesus' footsteps. If I keep my eyes on Him and stay on His straight path, I please Him. I am slow sometimes when it's time for me to move on because I do not stay focused. My mind is not stayed on Jesus constantly because the flesh is warring against the Spirit. No good thing dwells in the flesh. Jesus himself said the flesh does not please God. Jesus' disciples called him Good Master; He rebuked them saying that the flesh is of the earth.

TIME OF TRANSITION BY WAY OF KATRINA

I was planning, sometime in the future, to move to North Louisiana, maybe to Rayville where my property, the old Temple farmhouse is located. Evidently, my time was not in God's timing. His time was NOW! God's ways are higher than our ways; His thoughts are higher than our thoughts. He knows all things; nothing takes Him by surprise.

I was working my second job, starting at 2:00 o'clock P.M., at North Oaks Medical Center. I clocked in straight from my morning job at the candy company. I worked until I cleaned all my discharged patients' rooms. The staff encouraged us to speak to the patients to keep them comfortable and assure them of a pleasant stay. I enjoyed working at the hospital.

Pray about everything; worry about nothing. God closes one door and opens another. When you find favor with man, (the candy company owner), God has given us that favor. My Father knows the hearts of His children before we pray. Our hearts cry out to Him when we think we can't bear anymore. He hears and answers as we trust Him. He knows that our hearts' desires are centered on His plan, will, and purpose for us. We know that He has a time for everything in our lives. Everything is beautiful when it's God timing. Our planning and our timing are not God's plans or His timing. When we let go and let God's will, plan, and purpose for us be done, it is perfect for us every time. Jesus steps are slow; they are sure. He

always   arrive
on time. We must stay focused on Jesus and continue where He leads us; we will follow. We are not only called but we are chosen. The chosen obey God. His way is perfect. He makes everything beautiful in His time.

BETHANY'S TRIP TO GIBSLAND

I had no idea that the hurricane was changing its track from heading toward Florida toward New Orleans. My daughter and son-in-law had only been married a few weeks. Their plans were to pick me up from work and go to Ruston to get his work truck. They came to North Oaks Hospital where I worked, and we headed toward Gibsland. It was late in the night. The Interstate Highway was already busy with people evacuating. We drove several hours to my son Dion's home in Gibsland. We were surprised to see all of them up that late watching the news. When we walked in, they thought we had left Ponchatoula because of Katrina. We did not know that the hurricane had changed direction. We were surprised!

We had not taken extra clothes, nor baby items with us. We all sat down in the living room, stretched out on Dion's extra-long sectional sofa. The TV was the center of attention for the next month. All conservation was about Hurricane Katrina. Communication lines were down in the area. I tried to touch base with both of my jobs; there was no connection. This went on for a couple of weeks or more. When I did connect with them, the reports in Gibsland were that routes to Ponchatoula were not possible for traveling. I had some upset bosses. They thought I had run from Katrina. I had left for personal reasons, intending to make a fast trip back to Ponchatoula. I would have been back on the job with nobody knowing that I had left. Now we were stuck in Gibsland.

My daughter's baby was scheduled to be born soon. We had

a baby shower in Ponchatoula and all his things were there. We would have taken all our and the baby's things, if we had known the storm was going make landfall in Ponchatoula, when we left.

THE NEW BABY

It was close to the baby's birth. We made an appointment at Lincoln Memorial Hospital, Ruston, so that Shanara would be in their system. Since we were not from the area, we needed to be sure that our baby would have a place to be born. The ultrasound showed that he was a big healthy boy almost ready to meet his big family. On September 13, 2005, Shanara went into labor. My son Tony, Ashley, Grandma Nancy, and I attended this exciting event to welcome our bundle of joy!

We had a little surprise; the umbilical cord was around his neck. His doctor was a professional; she knew what to do. She eased her hand between the umbilical cord and the baby's neck and slipped the cord over his head. I thank God for saving the baby's life. Richard Scott Smith is our blessed baby. He was born with very black hair. Both his mom and dad have black hair. When going to the supermarket, children would ask if they could touch his hair. It was so soft and full of curls, beautiful! His biological dad did not want to marry. I did call him to let him know about the birth of the baby. He was in the Air Force National Guard with the rescue/cleanup crew. Our baby has a large Temple family who loves him. God loves all little children.

BETHANY'S TEMPORARY JOB

We needed an income. I thought I would get settled in getting a job in Gibsland. There were short-term temporary jobs which were offered by Katrina Work Force. I applied using my housekeeping custodial experience qualifications. I was offered a job with the Bienville Parish School System. I accepted the job working in Arcadia schools. My job was cleaning classrooms and working in the kitchen/cafeteria. They were fully staffed but made room for Katrina victims to help us financially. This was a blessing, but after working a few days, things started happening.

My van was parked on a slope near my son's carport. I did the unthinkable. I put the gear in reverse to back up; the tire appeared to be flat. Instead of shifting gear in park, I had my foot on the brake. I opened the car door to look at the tire. As I leaned out to look, my foot slid off the brake. When the van rolled backwards on to the road, I slid out of my seat and landed on the road. The front tire of my large custom-made van was sitting on both legs. The heavy weight on my legs caused my legs to be numb. I started screaming for someone to come and back the van off my legs. The tire on the back driver's side was off the rim. Amy came running outside and saw my legs under the tire. I told her to get in the van and back the van up, so the tire would free my legs. I told her that whatever she did, do not go forward because the heavy wheel with the rim exposed could cut through my legs. Thank God that Amy was calm enough to drive in the right direction. My son, Sidney, got a neighbor to help take me into the house. I could not work for some time because my ankles were extremely swollen, and it was difficult to wear shoes. Since we needed money to help with the household expenses, I tried to work. I do not like to depend on people. If possible, let us help each other.

    Early October, my niece, Lynette, passed away. She lived in Rayville. I had gotten a call from my sister a few days before her death. She wanted to go get Richard and wanted me to go visit with Lynette and Dorothy Rae. Lynette loved to rock babies in her rocking chair. Richard was a little less than one month old. It would have been a joy for her to be able to rock Richard. God knows all things. We did go to Lynette's; it was for her funeral, though. There I was, missing work again! I stopped in Ruston and bought four new tires with the money that I had earned on my job.

PRAYER WARRIORS TO THE RESCUE

I worked almost two straight months, October, and November. On December 6, 2005, I was in an automobile accident; the same day Dorothy Rae passed out when she fell and hit her head on the floor. Diane and Vincent seemed to always show up at the right place and the right time. They are pastors and praying ministers of the gospel. They are prayer warriors! They were in Rayville visiting and praying with Dorothy for her recovery. They were planning to leave soon from her house when they heard about my auto accident.

I got off work about 2:30, then had a short meeting. I always drove on the Interstate to and from work. I had not learned the Highway 80 route to go to work. I was on the Interstate driving home from work, on a clear day with little traffic, when my vehicle was hit on the back end of my van on the driver's side. I was holding the steering wheel tightly, as I always do. I feel more in control of my vehicle when holding tight to my steering wheel.

As the vehicle that hit my van continued hitting against my vehicle, it veered off the road. I was knocked unconscious with a concussion to my right temple. An ambulance took me to a medical center. I regained consciousness as we arrived at the emergency area. I had a clear loud thought as if I were speaking. My thought was "Why am I back, Lord?" Then my eyes opened, and I saw the paramedic standing over me. I asked him, "Where am I?" He told me that I was in an automobile accident and that we had just arrived at the Minden Medical Center. I did not feel any pain; I guess because my body was in shock.

My niece worked in the sheriff's department and informed my family of my accident. She went and stayed with me until my son, Dion, arrived. He was working at Fibrebond in Minden at the time. Minden Medical staff took care of my visible injuries. They cleaned and stapled the right side temple area. They also cleaned my right eye which was bleeding and swollen shut. The neck brace was applied at the accident site. My neck was broken, the left C-1 cervical. Six ribs on my right side were broken, which punctured my lungs. My left knee was cut open in a large L shape, exposing my bones. My knee was washed with a pressure hose. It was sutured except for an area for a drainage hose to be inserted. I was injured in my lower right kidney, which was bleeding.

About 9:00 P.M., the ambulance took me to LSU Hospital in Shreveport. My sister, Diane, and my brother-in-law, Vincent, arrived just in time to follow the ambulance. Immediately after the accident, I did not feel any pain. Now I felt every bump and every turn; I was in PAIN!

The stretcher that I was on was extremely hard. My broken ribs that punctured my right lung made it difficult for me to breathe. Diane and Vincent stayed beside me for two days praying for me. We need more prayer warriors like them. Prayer warriors are powerful weapons against the enemy.

Prayers are still going up to our Father. Prayer warriors are not those who come to your bedside and watch until the last breath leaves your body. They are fighting against Satan so he does not take the person's life early. We all have an important job to do for the Kingdom of God. There is no job too small. One breath makes the difference between Heaven and hell. God forgive me.

I was given a bed in the trauma ward. It was time for my body to move and walk so I could function when I got home. I still had my life before me to find God's will for the rest of my life. There is work to do to take care of my new grandson and God's work.

Dion had gone to the unit with me. He went as far he was allowed. He stood in the door of the hall by the room. A harness was brought to my room and hoisted it down to my bed. I could not move; they had to roll me from one side to the other to push the canvas under me so they could weigh me. They rolled me from the other side onto my back. The pain and soreness were so severe that I could not hold back my scream. I heard Dion crying in the hallway, calling someone to pray for me. The hoist lifted me up from the bed so the medics could weigh me. Dion went back home after that. I was discharged the following weekend. My children love their mother. They know that I am a true godly woman. They know that my prayers go up for them. I continued moving, walking to the bathroom. I was stiff a few days as my body was loosening up. I talked to my Father each day with the same words. I told him that I have never nor will ever suffer the pain and sorrows that He experienced on the cross for His love for all mankind. He suffered in agony; His sweat was as great drops of blood. The love of God is greater far, than any tongue can ever tell.

This was the end of my work force. My two daughters went to Family Services and signed us up for food stamps. We were approved with no problems. Now we could help the household with food. Dion's income would pay the bills but for a while it was a struggle. I was totally disabled and received Social Security Benefits; I could now raise Richard. His mom was ready to move back to Ponchatoula. Things never stay the same; changes take place with friends and places that you used to be familiar and comfortable with. Richard was a two-year-old when his mom moved. She was financially unable to take care of his needs. With some persuasion, I managed to get Shanara's approval to let him stay with us. She gave us temporary authority to take him to doctors appointments and enroll him in school. This was God's timing for me to be able to help with Richard while he was growing up. During this same time, I was able to help take care of Dexter until he graduated from high school in 2022.

RICHARD GOES TO SCHOOL

It was 2010, Richard was potty trained. When he was five years old, he started to Pre-K, early learning. He is very observant; he was very young when he started walking, about seven months old. He would watch other children when they sat down on the floor and when they would stand without holding onto anything. My sister, Dorothy, thought Richard was cute when he sat squatting on the floor. He first started using his hand on the floor to balance himself to stand up. When he started walking, Sidney held his little hand as they walked to the post office. His legs were strong; it wasn't long until Sidney had him walking further, to Fast Pak. Sid would buy him ice cream or candy before they walked back home. When he was in Pre-K, I remember that the teacher had a meeting with the school board counselors. Richard was a quiet child, especially, with people who he wasn't used to being around. His teacher thought that he might be autistic since he had not communicated with her nor the children in the class. She told me that when Richard walked into the meeting, he started talking about all the things he had learned in his classroom. The teacher told me that she could have cried as he was telling the group what he had learned. He is still very observant and when he does speak, he wants full attention. He is like a professor, very knowledgeable when he does speak. He is amazing! As Richard excelled in school, he has never been partial nor prejudiced. He did not see color. When the school got a new teacher or principal, he would say that he did not know what color they were. I would tell him that's okay. I did not try to explain because all people are the same. There are no differences. When you try to explain color, we are going against God's Word. We are all one people with God. We are all made from the dust of the earth. When he was about fifteen years old, Richard came home from school and said to me, "Nanny do you know that I am black?" I asked him who told him that he was black and he said that the kids at school told him. I told him that God's Word says that we are all His children and equal.

On ACT testing, he got high scores, exceeding most students. Some of his grades were the highest in his class. Richard graduated from high school on May 18, 2023, with great achievements, receiving scholarships to Louisiana Tech in Ruston. He will study Animal Science and plans to be a veterinarian. He hopes that the Animal Science studies will be at a university near his mother and siblings in South Caroline, for his specialized training.

MIRACLE INTERVENTIONS

My grandson, Dexter, was living with his mother and brother in Buras, Louisiana, south of New Orleans. Dexter's mom was rushed to the hospital because of seizures. He and his brother were home alone when this happened. A friend took them to the hospital and dropped them off, when she heard that I had arrived. A social worker had already called the Child Protection Service because the boys were dropped off at the hospital, even though I had told her that my family were on their way to the hospital to take the boys home with them. Shortly, a man arrived and introduced himself as being an Agent of the Child Protection Service. He said that he wanted to talk with Dexter, so he took him to a room alone. When they returned from the meeting, the Agent told me that he was taking Dexter to a family that could take care of him. He told Dexter that he would have fun playing video games and other fun things. I insisted that I had family members on their way to the hospital to take Dexter and his brother home with them. He then handed me his business card and let me know that the CPS had already put a claim in their system for Dexter. The Agent told me that I would be required to go through the Legal System to get him back.

About a month later, a date was set for me to go before the Judge with our petition. When that day arrived, the Agent and I went to the Judge's chamber and presented our complaint. The Judge was angry at the Agent for taking the matter into his own hands and removing Dexter from his family. The Agent apologized to us and to the Judge, saying that he will never remove another child without a detailed investigation. He learned his lesson!

A few weeks later, we returned to the Judge's chamber to hear his final decision on Dexter's situation. I went to his chamber with several others who were there to represent themselves and/or others. We sat around a long table where we were questioned and gave our responses. The Judge had spoken to Dexter earlier discussing his family home life. He told the Judge that he has a big family that loves him. The Judge presented his verdict. He ordered that Dexter be returned to his big loving family. The Judge gave his grandmother full custody of Dexter.

DEXTER'S MIRACLE DIPLOMA

This testimony is about my grandson, Dexter, who was diagnosed with autism, a neurological disorder. He's a very intelligent young man. He has mastered several subjects according to the state's tests results. Dexter worked very slowly doing his classwork due to his motor skills and other related issues. When he would get frustrated, he would shut down and not respond to instructions which upset his teachers and principal. They accused him of being deliberately stubborn, not wanting to do his work. The staff of his school got the Special Education Department involved and they labeled him as a bad behavioral problem child instead of admitting that he was autistic.

Our household was accused of being the cause of his behavior at school. They called our home numerous times, stating that we were the problem for allowing him to stay up late and play video games, which they said contributed to Dexter not being alert enough to complete his classwork.

I received a letter from the Special Education Department specifying a date, and an address, for Dexter and me to go to the Parish Courthouse. I thought this pertained to Dexter's education, but when we arrived, we were told to go to the Judge's office. I was wondering why we were there. A woman sitting at the Judge's desk immediately stated her name and began questioning Dexter. She asked him if he was involved in sex and pornography and if he wanted to kill a policeman, etc. Those were questions one would think that would be asked to a criminal suspect. I was startled! I immediately asked her why she was questioning my child about this subject. She told me that it was her duty because of the request from the Behavioral Department concerning Dexter. I informed her that Dexter is autistic, not criminal. We left that office shortly. I received calls and letters to return to the Courthouse for other meetings. I refused every time, stating that I would not sit there being accused of filth and lies. Through God's intervention with prayers from the church, family, and friends, things changed somewhat.

I sat in many IEP meetings listening to insults and accusations. I reminded the people that God sits high and looks low, observing all the matters of His children. Jesus said in Matthew 18:6, "Whoever harms my little ones, it is better for him that a millstone was hanged around his neck and drowned in the depth of the sea."

Dexter was in the twelfth grade; the time came for his graduation in May 2022. He needed to complete some of his courses to get the credits required for graduation. He worked tirelessly but slowly to complete his work. Graduation came, and he still needed to complete his requirements to walk with the class to receive his diploma. Through working hard, Dexter finished his required work. His work was graded, and he passed all subjects. I went to the principal's office and asked him to give Dexter a diploma. He and the teacher said that Dexter would not get a diploma but would get a certificate. I went to the school superintendent's office and told him that Dexter finished his work and received the credits necessary to earn a diploma. I informed him that I had spoken with the principal, letting him know that I wanted Dexter to have a diploma. He said that he would give Dexter a certificate, not a diploma. The superintendent stated that he has the authority to issue diplomas, not the principal. He said that Dexter would receive a diploma. Dexter's diploma was delivered directly into his little hands! When the principal said, no diploma, God said, signed, sealed, and delivered! We give God all the praises!

BETHANY'S TRIP TO ALABAMA

I had just bought a new 2007 Dodge Caravan. I had never been to Alabama for Bro. Phillip and Sis. Bonnetta Holloway's camp meetings. This church meeting trip was a good time to drive my new van to break it in. This camp meeting was in May 2007. Prior to this trip, I had a dream. In the dream, I saw my nephew, Gary, and his daughter, Jessica. I saw Gary as he told the family of a doctor's report that he had received about Jessica. He told us that she had a terminal disease/illness.

I had another dream while at Hilda's home sleeping on the sofa. We were going to leave early the next morning to go on our trip. I saw in my dream the inside of the Holloway's home and church; I had never been there. Terry Temple wanted to go to camp meeting with us, so we stopped in Rayville and picked him up. He and Hilda were our designated drivers; Dorothy Rae and I were the passengers.

We arrived in time for the evening service. We went inside the Holloway home and put our luggage in the bedroom that was provided for us. Then, we entered the living room where we visited their family until church time. As I glanced around the room, I said that I had seen their house before. Sis. Bonnetta said that I must have had a dream or vision because I had never been there before. Service time came to go into the church. I saw a picture of Bro. Willard and Sis. Mildred Holloway in the entrance of the church. Again, I saw something that was familiar to me; it was inside their sanctuary! You might say that when you enter a church that they all look alike. This church walls were painted light blue halfway and the other half was wood paneling.

We went inside the sanctuary as the service began. I was asked to sing. I sang a song that Bro. Jimmy Stewart from Tennessee had written. The title of the song is "Don't Give Up." I sang that song which had the name Daniel in it, as I looked toward Bro. Daniel and Sis. Betty Swinnea. When I sat back down in my pew, I overheard Bro. Daniel asking Sis. Betty who sang that song. She told him that I did.

The minister who brought the message that night went upon the platform and to the pulpit. I was glancing around to see if I knew anyone there other than the Holloways. Hilda was sitting next to me, and she began tapping my arm to get my attention. I looked at her and she told me to look at the preacher. When I looked at him, I knew what Hilda wanted me to see. I whispered to Hilda, "That man looks just like Gary Dean Bueltel"! This man looked as if he could be Gary's twin. I paid attention to him as he began his testimony. This not only looked like Gary, but his daughter was named Jessica! He continued his testimony. His daughter was diagnosed with a terminal illness, just like I saw in the dream. The preacher told how the Lord gave his daughter a supernatural miraculous healing. This trip was ordained by God; it was His divine will for us to be there. There were so many memories with the Holloway and Swinnea families. I remember when we went to the fellowship hall that Bro. Willard and Robert Holloway would sit down at the table with Dorothy and me. They told us of their memories of Bro. Irvin's miracles and the salvation messages. Bro. Willard had been going through Dialysis treatments. He told Dorothy and me that if Bro. Irvin was still alive that he would have been healed. One other thing that Bro. Willard told us, was that Bro. J.C. Swinnea told him that after Bro. Irvin died, that he winked at him from the casket. It meant that Dad was letting him know that all is well.

DOROTHY RAE PASSES

Dorothy Rae Temple Smith passed on December 25, 2007, in Arcadia, Louisiana. After a short illness and several trips to the doctor in Ruston, Dorothy was having more falls. I had spent a lot of time with Dorothy at Hilda's home. I was recuperating from my automobile accident in 2005. I was blessed to spend a couple of years getting to know more about my second oldest sister. We were married to Smiths; these Smiths were not related. I always heard that there are more Smiths and Joneses than any other names.

Dorothy made us her delicious famous chocolate tarts when she was able. Dorothy told me something interesting. She said that her favorite foods were hot dogs and Lay's plain potato chips and cocoa cola. There was something that she told me that was funny. An elderly cousin and her husband went to visit Dorothy. The cousin was telling us that she had never been touched by a man. My niece and I looked at each other as we glanced toward her husband. I went to Dorothy's hospital bed with her daughter. I asked her if she heard what our cousin said about never having been touched by a man. Dorothy spoke up with a strong voice, saying, "Don't you believe it!" Minta and I stayed with her until her 'home going'. Jane and Roger had arrived just in time, prior to her passing. Her departure was on Christmas Day! She went to meet Jesus on His birthday. What a celebration it must have been!!

BETHANY'S STREET MINISTRY ON HIGHWAY 80 IN GIBSLAND, LA

Richard Scott Smith, who Sidney Lynn Smith (Poppa) raised from birth, September 13, 2005, in Lincoln Parish Hospital, Ruston, Louisiana, started to Pre-K Early Learning Center in 2010. I had been writing my Stay Focused Bible messages by hand since 2008. I had two or three pages, front and back that I would send by mail to 30 Temple households.

Sheri bought me a copier/printer a few years later. It was a blessing to me to be able to copy 30 messages from one hand-written copy. This was amazing! See how God works? It was a long time after getting the copier machine that my sister bought my first tablet. With this tablet, I learned to text my Stay Focused messages. I can now send 60 messages. Wow! God is good!! I had plenty of spare time and started writing a book about my mom and dad's life. I had forgotten about the book for a while.

I went into a more personal and physical way in ministering to people. My first street ministry started outside in front of Dion's house, sitting in my swing that Tony and Ashley had bought me for Mother's Day. My van was parked in the driveway. It was a good place to display the poster boards on the windows of the van. I wrote on the back and the front of the posters, saying, "Jesus loves you. Repent for the Kingdom of God is at hand. Jesus is coming soon," etc. I wrote these few words to get to the point. I used a black marker and wrote in big letters so they could be seen from the street. I taped them on the windows of my vehicle. As people drove by, I would wave at them.

      I went to Gibsland City Hall and introduced myself to the mayor. I told him that I wanted to do Street Ministry, maybe at the Community Center property. He approved my request. The Center was used for special occasions only. I would take a chair with me and put it near the building with my Bible on it. I parked my car near the street and taped all my signs on all the windows. My location was between the Post Office and the Fast Pak. The location was ideal for my ministry. People would walk by either going to the Post Office or the store and I would minister to them. Those who drove by would drive slowly and read the signs or some would stop near the building. I would go to their vehicle window and speak to them. They had various prayer requests for me to pray about; some were praying for their bodies, their ministries, their job, etc. The Lord blessed in this endeavor, doing the Lord's work for two years in that area.

BETHANY'S STREET MINISTRY IN RAYVILLE AREA

In 2012, I ended my street ministry in Gibsland because my nephew, Joshua, who lived in Rayville was reported missing. Sidney helped his family searching the area where his truck was located. I would go back and forth to send Richard to school. At this time, I decided to go into Walmart to ask permission to do street ministry in their parking lot. I parked away from the store at the end of their parking lot. I would cover my van with the posters. We ministered there several weekends as our family was searching for Josh.

The first day of my Rayville ministry was in Delhi, east of Rayville, for one day. I drove to Brookshire's parking lot and spoke to the manager about doing street ministry outside. He said it was okay. I parked near the street so I wouldn't interfere with the customers. Some shoppers would stop by to listen to my miracle testimonies. Again, I had the large poster messages on my vehicle. On the second day, I had planned to minster in Start, west of Rayville. I drove to the small community of Start, Louisiana. My mom, dad, and other Temple relatives are buried at the Start Cemetery. I went to the store and told the man behind the counter that I would like to minister outside. I let him know that I would be out of the way of the store and not hinder his business. He said to me, "No mam!" I asked to speak with the manager, he said he is the manager. I let him know that my parents were buried in the cemetery near the store. He let me know with his arm stretched out that the store and property was owned by him. I said, "Great! So, you can allow me to minister beside the tree out of the way of the store customers.". Again, he said to me, "No mam!" I told him that Jesus is a witness against this day by not allowing His word to go forth. I thought that I would have to go back to Rayville Walmart to minister. About halfway to Rayville, the Holy Spirit spoke to me to go to the Rayville courthouse. God is great! I parked behind the courthouse and went inside as I saw an open door to my left. Above the door was a sign indicating that it was the tax accessor's office. I walked inside, there were two ladies. I introduced myself, letting them know that I am a Christian woman and that I do street ministry. I told them that I needed to speak with someone in authority to give me permission to minister near the courthouse. They told me I would need to go to the sheriff's office. After talking with them and witnessing, I walked to the other end of the hall and went into the office on my right where they told me to go. Some ladies were in that office, and I told them about the miracles that happened in my Temple family. I was told to go to the basement down the hall where the sheriff's office was located. There were several deputies there but no sheriff. I told them why I was there.

    I told the deputies that I would like to speak to the sheriff about having street ministry on the courthouse lawn. I was told that they do not allow that because too many people would want to do the same thing. He continued explaining that there would be too much traffic on the streets and property. Deputy Odom told me to go across the railroad tracks. The Police Department was straight across the street. He said the Police Chief would be the next in authority when the sheriff was not available.

MY STREET MINISTRY ON HIGHWAY 80 – RAYVILLE

I went to the Police Department, on Highway 80, the main street. Would you believe that God does not have accidents, incidents nor coincidences. They are God's will for His chosen ones. This was the same Highway 80 in Gibsland where I started the street ministry.

I parked there and went inside the office; I told the lady at the desk that I would like to speak to the Police Chief. A few minutes later I was shown to his office. Chief Willie Robinson told me to go in and take a seat. I introduced myself and let him know that I am a Christian; he told me that he is also a Christian and Deacon in his church. He was very cordial, and I testified to him about my dad's conversion from an alcoholic to a born again Christian. I told him that God had chosen Dad to preach the Gospel of Jesus Christ. I let him know that Dad was given the gifts of healings and miracles; and God used him in casting out demons. I told Chief Robinson that Dad had ministered on the streets of Rayville.

We had a nice lengthy conversation. I mentioned to him about going to the Courthouse to find out if I could minister on that property. The Sheriff was not available, so the deputy referred me to you. The Chief of Police told me that no one ever had ministered on the Court House property nor on the streets. He said that on Veterans Day they usually have a program honoring the veterans on the Courthouse lawn. He mentioned that Walmart and Brookshire's usually allow people to minister on their parking lots. I told him that I had ministered a few times there during 2012. I said to him that I would go back to that area.

Immediately, the Chief said that he had a place for me near his office. He told me about the old, abandoned service station that was between Napa and the café. I was overjoyed with this offer! I asked him if it was privately owned, and he said that it is. I said that you must own it; he said no, but he knows who does and that he would not mind my using it. I told him that I appreciated what he was doing for me. I thanked him for blessing me with a place to minister the Word of God.

Chief Robinson called about eight names of policemen to come into his office. He told his crew that I was going to minister next door to their building. He told them he wanted me, Sis. Temple, to pray for their department. They gathered near his desk as I asked everyone to join hands. They did and the Holy Spirit prayed through me. All the police officers returned to work except one. That young policeman walked with me to the next block from City Hall. He showed me the designated area where I could set up my ministry.

The date was October 9, 2014, Thursday. This day was certainly ordained by God. I witnessed to more people on that day in Rayville. I believe there were about 20 people total that I witnessed to then. Chief Robinson had given to me his business card to show to anyone who tried to be troublemakers. During that day of ministering, all those people heard the miracles that had taken place in our G.I. Temple Family. Some of the miracles included the Tornado of 1953, my vision being restored, and Jimmy DeVonne's thumb accident. The ministry continues.

BETHANY "TEMPLE OF GOD"

I believe our entire G.I. Temple and Margaret Florene Wilson Temple Family are not just called but chosen by God. We are set apart for God's will be done in and through us. Now it is high time to wake up, repent and obey God. Keep on the firing line; they who endure to the end shall be saved. It doesn't matter how long ago that you started, the important thing is to finish what was started to the end. Let us get back on track and redeem the time that we have lost. Let us work while it is day for night (darkness) comes when no one can work.

|2012 – JOSHUA IS MISSING

I stopped the ministry in Gibsland in 2012 when my nephew was reported as being missing. Sidney and I went to my hometown in Rayville to help search for Josh. The area where his truck was found was where they focused on searching for him. I went back and forth from there to Gibsland so Richard could stay in school. During those weekends, Richard and I parked away from the Walmart and Brookshire's stores, taped the posters on the van and ministered there for several weekends as the search for Joshua continued.

A few years later, as I was helping Sidney to get his driver's license, there was a block preventing him from obtaining a license. I went to the Sheriff's office in Arcadia, introduced myself, to let him know why I was there. I told him that Sidney needs his license to drive me to take care of my business. As he searched the computer, he saw that Sidney's identification was being used by someone else. Sidney never had a driver's license. He asked if Sidney had ever had another identification. I told him that Sid only had one that I was aware of. Then, the Sheriff told me something very interesting. He said that more than likely, he is still out there somewhere, meaning, that whoever had Sidney's identity was no longer using it but using a different identity.

2017 CAMPMEETING AND BEYOND

Camp meeting was always the last of the school year. The last week of May the family and visitors would go to the campgrounds. The building was full to capacity and sometimes overflowing. There were buildings with many places for the people to sleep.

There was lots of preaching, praying, singing, shouting, and praising God. The altars were full of people on both sides, crying out to the Lord. Yes, the enemy was always present to hinder the services. He comes on God's Holy property; he is a bold devil when he comes inside God's House. Either the devil will be cast from God's House or God, himself, will leave. If the leaders do not repent, nor give sacrifice of praise to God in this matter, they will be judged and corrected, or their candle will be removed! Read Revelations 3, the messages to the seven churches of Asia. Those revelations that happened back then are the same revelations for our churches today. Wake up church or you will realize that God is no longer in your church. Everything you do will be operating from your flesh and not of the Holy Spirit.

REMEMBERING THOSE WHO HAVE GONE ON

With the missing of Joshua Charles Berry, I'm still believing of his miraculous return at such a time as this. (Missing in 2012.) A chain of events has taken place. The passing of Ronnie Charles Smith to his resting place until the great resurrection day. His passing occurred on Arbor Day, April 26, 2013. Prior to his death, I came to visit with Ronnie in April. I had written my first song, The Sixth to Ninth Hour, as well as a few other songs. I remember telling Ronnie about these songs as I sang and read some of the words to him. He told me that they were beautiful songs. The passing of James Roy Antee was November 25, 2013. The passing of Roy Henry Antee, Copastor with his wife, was on August 23, 2014. Next, was the passing of Jonathan Phillip Antee-Morris on October 15, 2020. The passing of Hilda Jean Smith Antee was on January 15, 2021. The passing of Lizzie Mae Temple Hernandez was on December 27, 2020. The passing of William Byron Temple was August 31, 2022.

BETHANY TRYING TO UNDERSTAND WHAT'S HAPPENING WITH HER

The Word of God is the only true Word of Prophecy. It is God telling us what has happened before, will happen again. There is nothing new under the Heavens. It has happened in the beginning and comes to earth as if we have seen it before. It is called foreknowledge. God knows all things; He created all things. He now shows His children in dreams, visions, and thoughts. God is giving us a picture of our lives before it happens. He teaches us as He leads and guides us along our path.

December 11, 2022, on Sunday at 1:30 A.M., I was trying to figure out the spiritual warfare that I am in. It is not so much a physical battle, but it can make your body tired! It is Spiritual warfare that I am in. A Word that I had received from the Lord was, "Let Go and Let God." Worry about nothing, pray about everything! Do not lean to my own understanding but acknowledge God and He will direct my path. I was trying to figure out to understand what I was going through. That is why God gave me this message.

Since January 2022, I have been communicating with My Friend. This was through our mobile phone's signals, symbols, playing games, and messaging was not as clear an understanding as talking. Our friendship and courtship started through our phones. We seemed to enjoy and were satisfied with this type of relationship of being together. My Friend had opposition from his family because of our race differences.

I told him from the beginning that when I was ready to meet him that I do not want any touching, nor sex. I said that those things are for marriage. He replied to me saying, that I was a blessed woman of God. He chose not to meet me. I found out why we never met. He let me know that he was concerned about our meeting in person. He wanted to respect my wishes. As of this time, 2023, we have not met in person. We will meet if it's God's will. I told him that when we do meet if anything happens, we will do the right thing by getting married. Marriage is honorable and the bed is undefiled, but whoremongers will have their part in the lake of fire. I told him that I do not want to get into a sinful situation. I believe that it is God's will for us to be married, husband and wife. I could have dated other men, but I did not want to give place to the devil. The saying goes that if you give him an inch, he will take a mile. I abstained from situations that I knew could lead to sin. I do know without a doubt, that God knows all things and that His will, plan, and purpose will be done at this time in my life. It is no longer my will but God's will for my life for as long as I live. Patience is a major factor in honoring God's will, way, and His timing! We must let patience have its perfect work so we will be entire and have want for nothing. God was trying to get through to me when He gave me those simple words, 'Let go; let God'. That is when He reminded me to pray about everything and worry about nothing. I slacked off communicating with my friend. It was not long before he started talking more seriously about a meeting date. He also talked about a wedding date. See how God works. There is a time and a season for everything under the Heavens. Let go; let God.

BETHANY'S NEW BEGINNING – MY TRANSITION

I have been praying for direction in my life. My two grandsons whom I helped raise were finishing high school. I knew I still had work to do for the Kingdom of God. I was born to serve the Lord. According to my age, I believe this transition time would most likely be my final. I just turned 71, July 17, 2021. Both numbers with the number one means the beginning of my perfection, my victory over death, hell, and the grave with Jesus Christ for eternal life. Psalms 90:10, says the days of our years are three score years, 70; and ten equals 80, if by reason of strength and health, they will be four score years meaning 80. Yet is their strength, labor, and sorrow for it is soon cut off, and we will fly away to our eternal home.

Our Temple Family Reunion had just started July 2021. My spirit was heavy knowing that I had to make a transition. Things and life itself bring about change in our lives. This change when you get older makes you wonder what can I do for God now? Changes in a person's life are bittersweet moments.

My heart felt heavy and troubled not knowing what God's will, plan, and purpose was for me. I could not hold back my tears. I carefully arose from the table where I was sitting in the fellowship hall. I walked next door to my sister's home. She and another sister knew my troubled spirit. I did not know that they were watching me. I knelt by the sofa and cried out to God. I heard other voices praying and crying out to God with me. We were all asking God for direction for my life. The other voices were my two sisters crying out to God for me. The Holy Spirit is my Comforter, my Leader, my Guide, and Teacher who lifted me up. My sisters and I walked back to the fellowship hall. Not long afterward, I was back in my chair with the family and friends. My son Tony walked over and sat down beside me. He began talking to me and said a man that he worked with wants to meet me. This man was soon to retire and wanted a wife to enjoy his life with. He said the man liked eating out traveling, and fishing. The man has a daughter who lives in Texas. I interrupted my son and reminded him that I'm 71 years old and that I'm too old to marry again. I have been single 20 years; I did not want to get married. Tony said that he told the man my age; the man was 61. He was not concerned about my age. I told Tony that I was not interested. He said, "Well I gave his message to you; can I give him your phone number?" I said, "Okay,"without thinking. Just that one short answer, "okay," started something that I could never believe in my wildest dreams. What would transpire in my simple everyday life is unheard of, especially in our modern times.

Just a few days later, August 9, 2021, I received a call from this mystery man. He repeated the things that Tony had told me. I repeated to him the same words that I told Tony saying that I did not want a man in my life nor marriage. I asked him if he would like me to keep his number and add him to my Stay Focus Messages. He said that would be okay. He said that he would like to send me a picture of himself. I let him know that he looked okay, but that I was still not interested in having a man in my life, now. My thoughts were why would I want to be married now; I have been single for several years. I sent the picture to my sister and told her that it looks like I've seen this man somewhere before.

I began sending him Stay Focus Messages. He would comment with very few words. He would text Amen, okay or that's right. Every now and then I would text him that I was still praying for God to bless him with a wife. He would text back thank you. Sometimes I would text him to say do not grow weary that God would send him a wife. One time I asked him if he wanted a girlfriend or a wife. He texted back saying that he did not want a girlfriend. He said that he prayed to God that he wants his own wife. He seemed upset or offended at that point. I began to tell him about my bad marriage. I told him that God is my best friend. The Bible says that He is friend that sticks closer than a brother. God will never let us down. He began to say that God is who he goes to for answers. I told him not to give up that God will give him what he asks for according to His will, plan, and purpose for his life. I told him that God does these things in His own time, not ours.

September 20, 2021, I could feel that he was happy. I texted him and asked him if God was showing him anything. He texted back saying, "Got to be watchful". I replied that was a wise thought. He answered with a thank you. I texted him saying that he must be happy; I guess maybe because he got rested from working. I reminded him that everything is in God's timing. He texted back with an amen. In the same text at the end of the message I texted him that I had been thinking about you more than usual. He replied, "Thank God". I was wondering why this man was saying thank God. I read over my message to him; there was the odd comment! Why did I text such a message to him? That was the message that this man was waiting for. I pondered on the unusual comment that I sent to this stranger. A rush of love flowed through me for this man. I had never experienced a strong passion of love before.

I believe that it was from God. I was surprised, myself. The love remained in my heart. The love kept growing as I sent his Stay Focus Messages to him. They became more personal to me at this time. I had not met him in person; we did not have conversations, nor personal text messages. How could this have happened to me? I talked to the Lord. The Holy Spirit reminded me of my July prayers and cries that went up to Him. I wanted God's perfect will, plan, and purpose for the rest of my life. Soon after crying, praying to the Lord, my son told me about this same man.

Next, he texted that he wanted to meet me. This time I replied that I was ready to meet him. I let him know that I did not want any touching nor sex. He did not text back right away. I texted him letting him know that touching and sex are for marriage. He then texted that you are a blessed woman in Jesus Christ. As I write this, April 6, 2023, I still have not met my friend in person.

The latter part of 2021, I asked him if he loved me. He let me know that he did not know because he had never seen me. I texted him saying that I have not seen God, but I love him. I thought that my son had sent a picture of me to him. He said the picture he received was of a group of people and he didn't know which one was me. I sent some pictures of me to him.

I remembered a vision/dream that I had about six months to a year before all of this happened. This is the dream: there was a building with a tall ceiling. I saw a tall man and a woman standing beside him at the far end of the building to my right. I had opened two large doors of the building as I walked in and saw them standing there. I had told my sister at that time about this dream. She asked was that all I saw, and I said that was all.

In March 2022, I received a call from a young woman and did not recognize the number. I didn't answer because I thought it was a wrong number. I received text messages a few days later from the lady asking who I was. I gave her my name and Stay Focus Message information. I asked her name which I did not recognize. The Holy Spirit revealed to me that this young lady was the one that I had seen with the man in my dream. She must have gotten my phone number from her dad's phone. I told her at the beginning about my dream of her and her dad. I had not ever heard of him or her. I told her about my son giving me the message that her dad had sent for me. I texted her that same message that her dad had given to my son to give to me. The Lord revealed to me her part in my dream which was that she thought I wanted their property if we married. I told her what the Lord showed me. She said that I knew more than what I told her. I let her KNOW that all I know is what God reveals to me. I began to minister to her, telling her that she has visions and dreams. I told her that God wants to use her to tell others the visions and dreams that she has. She let me know that she used to have visions and dreams, but not anymore. I do believe that this lady did not want her dad to marry anyone.

September 21, 2021, I went to bed; I woke up at about 12:30 A.M. on September 22, 2021, and went to the bathroom. When I laid back down, I couldn't go to sleep; I started to talk to the Lord, and He began to bring things to my mind. I remembered that my grandson had told me that I did not look 70 years old. He had seen people who were talking about their age who were younger than 70 and he said that they looked much older than I did. This is something I was concerned about because my friend is much younger. That comment was encouraging. I guess I got God's attention by Him reminding me that I might appear to be about the same age as this man. Maybe no one would notice that I am older.

    I want to fulfill God's will in my life. I had begun to feel lonely and sad because I wanted to stay busy doing God's work. I believe that this man who I was rejecting but still contacting him through my Stay Focus Messages could be God's will. His steps are slow, but they are sure. He might not come when we want Him, but He is always on time. During the meantime, I had to keep walking by faith, one step at a time. A person needs lots of patience with their faith. I have found that I lack patience. Especially, during these two full years, with many thoughts in my mind, wondering why God's will, plan, and purpose still has not come to fruition.

    A couple of dates were set for us to meet, which fell through to disappointments. We cannot make things happen. God must have His perfect will so we will be entire and having want for nothing. When we wait upon the Lord, He will renew our strength. We shall run and not grow weary; we shall walk and not faint; we shall mount up with wings like eagles. I told my friend that God makes everything beautiful in His timing. He texted to me that you are right. I texted him and told that I am in love with Jesus. He is my Lord, my God, my Holy Spirit, Whom I love with all my heart, mind, body, soul, and spirit. I also do love my neighbor as myself. The Holy Spirit is my Comforter, and He is always near me. The Bible says if we say that we love God and hate our neighbor, we are a liar. I am married to Jesus; I trust Him. He says do not put your trust in man, people; we would be disappointed. My friend texted me again saying that you are right. Jesus knows what's best for us. Amen. I texted him saying, "Be blessed."

My special friend and I are messengers of God. I am excited to get on with our last step to be together as husband and wife. It has been two long years. I always thought that I had lots of patience and was strong spiritually. This two-year journey has been rough and tiring, not only in the spirit but in the flesh. My book writing has been a blessing to me; it has kept me busy. During those times, things seem to have gone fast. We have not met personally, purposely staying away from our meeting. That was a wise decision. We want to wait for our wedding day. At one point in time, I told him that our lives are Biblical. I even told him that we are an old couple like Abraham and Sarah. Our wedding is scheduled in July, but what year?? He wants to work more hours before we get married. He wants us to have more time to spend together.

I am excited this is April 7, 2023, Good Friday. I just received a message from the publisher of my book, G.I. Temple – Soldier of Faith and the Pearl. She said the book was completed and ready for shipment. It is beautiful! She did a professional job. Look at Jesus! This good news is on crucifixion day! "It is finished!" Jesus, said. How Biblical is that?? My book is finished!

God knows all things; He knows the secrets of our hearts. We cannot hide anything from Him. My secret heart's desire is to have my own husband who truly loves me for real. I always wanted a compassionate husband to give me passionate loving kindness that I have never experienced. Husbands are usually about jumping into bed and out.

    You can see another aspect of this regarding our children who want nourishing, kindness, gentleness, and love. Instead, some children are cursed, mistreated, beaten, and abused. That is all they know. How sad this is! Jesus loves the little children. My heart cries out for them. I'm believing that this man who God is giving to me is my heart's desire. We will be an example of God's love to those that we minister to. This is just the beginning of April 2023. God is always on time, and even though My Friend has not retired yet. We have gone through many difficulties; we have passed the test. Our faith in God is what has brought us through this day. Our strength was in knowing that God has chosen us for such a time as this. God is looking for someone, anyone who will let God's will in their lives to be done.

    We cannot continue in the same cycle that we have been going through. We are getting older and have set dates before that have not come to fruition. God has all things in His hands. We know that the enemy is allowed to try to hinder God's will. We grow weary at times. Satan tried his best at Job; God's man always overcomes when oppositions come our way. My friend and I have made the same statements at different times during this journey. If we are meant to be husband and wife, God's will shall be done. When in God's will, there is no gossip nor confusion; the talking between one another brings confusion. This stopped our set date earlier. This time we have kept our wedding date confidential until the time to release it. This is not just about our marriage but it's about God's will, plan, and purpose for His Kingdom, souls being saved. We cannot lean to our own understanding. It's not good to confide in best friends. Look at

Job's friends. They were confusing and guessing all things that could be wrong adding to his problems and his misery. The Bible says to be swift to hear and slow to speak. This is the wisdom that God wants for His children in all matters concerning their lives. Finally, I told My Friend that he is the one who can make our wedding happen because he had asked God for a wife. It is his place to plan everything according to his work schedule. He is a hard-working man. God's timing is what's important in the end.

MY TEMPLE FAMILY HAS RESPECT FOR ALL PEOPLE

From a child, we would visit other churches. This was a time when churches were burned to the ground. The hatred racist people who thought they were doing God a favor, are currently saying that they are Christians; but they are liars. God is love. The Church, God's Church, are the ones who will arise to meet the Lord in the air. Some people will wonder on that day why they did not rise to meet Jesus. Richard did not see color; he saw all people the same – just people. About three years ago, he came home from school asking me if I knew that he is black. I said no that I did not know that he was black. He said that some kids at school told him that he is black. The people who see color are the ones who have the problem with racism. Why can't we see through God's eyes? There would be no division. Let us be one in Jesus Christ; let us unite in our faith in Jesus, bringing forth unity before some get left behind. On the day that we stand before the Lord and we say that I prophesied in your name, I healed the sick in your name, I did this, and I did that in your name, God will say, "Depart from me, you workers of iniquity, I never knew you".

Father Abraham was a dark-skinned man; his wife Sarah was a fair-skinned woman. Moses was married to an Ethiopian woman; his sister was rebuked for her remarks regarding Moses' wife. Man was made from the earth; woman was made from man's rib. There are different shades of skin; inside all are flesh colored alike. As people multiply, there are many skin color shades. We are all one in Jesus Christ. At the tower of Babel,

God saw all were one people and one language. He came down and confused their language, so they couldn't understand one another. This is when the people scattered throughout the earth. It was a time of division and confusion. Now is the time for God's people to unite as one in Christ Jesus. I am glad that My Friend chose me to be his wife. Only those who see color or nationality do not know God's Word nor His love. Even in our Constitution, it states that all men are created equal. Evil leaders changed our Godly laws. Satan has gotten into top leadership to bring down America. Satan wants control. Perhaps it is God's purpose to show certain people who have trouble believing that God created all mankind in His image. It is not to divide but to unite, especially, for those that are in His Church. This does not mean that everybody should marry in their own race; love is what should unite people in marriage.

This understanding is for God's true Church that there are neither black nor white, Jews or Gentile, neither male nor female. We are all one in Christ. God created all of us in His image. Read God's Word. God says to all men, that when they find a wife, he finds a good thing. He finds favor with God and man. God is the one and only God; He is the creator of all things. He made everything beautiful in His time; He saw that it was good.

PREPARING TO BE THE BRIDE

God has chosen and blessed me to honor Him as His bride. I will cherish and obey Him as my head and my covering. Jesus Christ is the head of His church. What an honor we have as we prepare for that beautiful, glorious occasion.

I had no idea what was unfolding in my life here on earth. I want God's will, plan, and purpose for my life, seeking His directions. Then a man, My Friend, showed up seemingly out of nowhere. God knows all things, the beginning, and the end. My Friend wanted a wife. Somehow, I was chosen to be his wife. This was an unusual journey that I was chosen to fulfill. Was God testing me? Was He allowing Satan to come against me to prove to Satan that whatever he came against me with, I would stay true to my faith in Jesus Christ?

I am a willing vessel for God. His love for me is far greater than any tongue can ever tell. I do love God with all my heart, soul, body, and spirit. I love my neighbor as myself. I say Jesus use me; please do not refuse me. Surely, there is work in your Kingdom that I can do. Even though my work is humble, let my will crumble. Though the cost be great, I'll work for you, even to my death.

My Friend saw no color, but his family was against him dating or marrying a white woman. He let them know that whatever happens will be. I wanted to know what God's purpose was for me in marrying this man or any man. The Lord let me know that in His Kingdom we are as the angels. We do not marry nor give in marriage. God's will, His purpose is always about souls added to His Kingdom; empty hell and fill Heaven. God filled my heart with love for this man. From that moment I was ready to be his wife, not his girlfriend. God moves in His time and season, not mine, nor yours, nor My Friend's. His steps are slow, but they are sure. When He arrives, He will make all things beautiful in His time.

There was nobody that I could pour my heart out to. I did not want to get anyone involved in what God was revealing to me concerning my life. I wanted the Holy Spirit to lead, guide, and direct me through my new transition. I knew including anyone could be an obstacle in my way instead of helping.

When someone prepares for such an important event, such as marriage, usually there is a best friend to help. My best friend is the Holy Spirit. He knows more about me than anyone. We must walk slowly as He helps with every step that we make. We cannot lean to our own understanding; we are in a spiritual warfare. In everything, we must acknowledge Him and He will direct our paths.

BETHANY'S OPEN VISIONS

I had some amazing wonders to occur as I continued following the Holy Spirit. I moved as He would move me. The first thing that I did was to go visit my doctor. It was early one morning just as his office was opening for patients to go in. I did not have an appointment. I signed in at the front desk. I told her that I had two skin tags that I needed to have removed. The doctor called me into the examination room; his assistant had the instrument that was needed for this procedure. I was in and out of the room by the time his appointed patients were ready to see him. That is how my God works!

Next, I made an appointment to have my missing front tooth to be replaced. I had to wait a month before the doctor could see me. This was totally different from my doctor's visit. After my visit with the dentist, I was scheduled to go back after another month. Again, this was slow, taking time, unlike my doctor's visit. I could sense interference with the dentist's appointments and visits. The enemy was stepping in, slowing things down. He was trying to frustrate me to make me weary.

While in town, I went to a department store and bought some items. The store that I entered had a Grand Opening Banner outside. There was no sign with the name of the store. While I was checking out, my sister called and asked what I was doing. I told her that I was checking out, paying for my things. My phone was on speaker as she asked me what the name of the store was. As I looked around for the name, the people chimed in that the store was Beall's. By that time, I had noticed on the burgundy wall above the door the word 'Beall's, written in lower case, cursive letters. I repeated to my sister that the store was Beall's; she asked Belk's; I said, no, that it was Beall's. I paid for my things and left the store.

The next month, I went for my dental visit. Dr. Bell, my dentist, was not in the office. The visit was with the hygienist to clean my teeth. I asked her why Dr. Bell was not in because she was supposed to start working on my teeth. The hygienist said that she would be out for a while, so I asked if she had Covid. I was told that she did not have Covid and would be back. The receptionist called several days later letting me know to find another dentist. She gave me a list of several dentists who could help me. I chose to go to Ringgold. I called to find out if they do bridge work. The answer was yes, so I made an appointment.

While I was in town, I went to Beall's department store and purchased some items. I asked for the discount that should apply to my purchase. She asked for my receipt, but I couldn't find it. When I told her that I had shopped there, she told me that the store is Burke's Outlet, not Beall's. Now, there was no Dr. Bell nor Beall's department store! What was going on? Dr. Bell could just get up and leave, but a store could not just disappear. Several times later when I went back to town, I would search for Beall's; Burke's Outlet was there.

The time had come for me to go to Ringgold for my dental appointment. I was seen immediately. The second visit was only a week later. The receptionist told me that all the patients that were scheduled were given new appointments. The last half of the scheduled day was for the doctor to complete his work bridging my new tooth. By the end of the workday, at 5:30, my dental work was completed. It was a beautiful job, well done. I did not have to wait and no reason to return. Again, see how our God intervenes.

My Second Open Vision

Another open vision that I had was when I was lying down resting, a large span of the most beautiful small blue flowers came down from Heaven and sat down beside me. The wind from the flowers descending blew my hair. The fragrance of the flowers was like I would think a heavenly aroma would be. The color was vivid and brilliant, too. These visions that I literally saw could only be from God. He was showing me to let me know that He was well pleased. It was confirmed to me that I was going through something spiritual and natural.

My daughter-in-law had remembered that I had told her and my son about the open vision that I had about Beall's department store. On May 17, 2023, my daughter-in-law let me know that Burke's Outlet store had changed its name to Beall's. They were amazed.

GOD'S BLESSINGS ON ME

On Christmas the year 2021, I was blessed with money from my family. I purchased two new purses to take to church. I lost a few pounds that I hope I do not regain; I feel much better health wise. I bought a few clothes that fit better and gave the larger ones to the church. I was blessed with new dress shoes. The Holy Spirit was leading me as I was preparing to be a wife. It's all about souls being saved for the Kingdom of God. I believe there are others who are crying out to God for help in their lives. I believe that the area God has chosen me to work in for His Kingdom is where the people are crying out to Him for help. This is harvesting time. There is much work to do, but few people that are willing to work in His field. Get out of your comfort zone; time is running out. Get busy for the Kingdom of God is at hand. Many are called but few are chosen. Only the chosen will obey. This is an address change, notification! We are moving to our brand-new home.

BETHANY'S AND SPECIAL FRIEND'S MESSAGES FROM MARCH 2023 – CURRENT

My special friend and I have pet names for each other. He calls me wife and I call him husband when messaging each other. His messages to me usually begin with, Husband and Wife are you and me. These are some messages that we sent to each other from March 7, 2023, to current. My messages to him each day usually start with, good morning, Sweet Heart. I love you Brother. You are my sweetheart man of God that I love; hugs and kisses.

You are the only man that I truly love. This love came from God. Husband and wife love each other. Our wedding is your decision, so do whatever you want in making it happen. I believe that the man is the head of the house. You make our decisions; what you say is our final answer. I do appreciate you, honor you, and respect you. I will not argue with you. I will not talk about you with anybody. You and I will be one. Yes, I do love you very much, my special friend. You have a blessed day in Jesus Christ.

My special friend says that husband and wife are you and me. He said on March 12, 2023, "We will have a wedding. The only ones that will be there for the wedding will be you and me." I said, "Yes, okay."

On March 13, he said that we are going to have a wedding in July. I let him know that I did not want anything to go wrong with our wedding.

I was listening to a new song. The title is "Address Change Notification." I will have an address change notification.

He said, "Husband and wife are you and me. We are going to have a wedding in July, and I want you to come to my house, and then we will go to the church."

I told him, "Yes, okay, wow, thank you!"

On March 18, he said that I want you to know that I have been thinking about you.

I said, "Okay, Sweet Heart. I love you."

On March 20, he said, "That I want you to be able to move in with me when we are married."

I said okay and that I will have all of my things in my van.

On March 22, he said that he would get some time off from work for the wedding so we would have more time to be together.

I said, "Okay. Have a blessed night."

He told me that I am the only one that he loves so much. I am going to be with you for the rest of my life.

I said, "Thank you so much. That's what I love to hear."

On March 23, he said that he was going to be able to get more work on the weekends.

I said, "Okay."

On March 26, he said that he was going to be able to move on to the next step to make sure that everything is done correctly by July.

I said, "Okay, yes".

He said to me, I can give you a little more information about what I want you to do for me and my family; it's very important to me. When we go out to dinner with my family and friends, this is what I want you to know about me. When I get a chance to talk about you and your family, this is the best way for us to get to know you.

I said, "Okay, yes, thank you for helping me to know what is expected of me."

On April 18, he said to me, Bethany, you know that I love you so much and I want to be with you forever. I will never forget what you are doing for me. When we go out to dinner with the family, it's going to be fun.

I said, "Okay."

BETHANY JOYCE TEMPLE

|THE REVALATION THAT GOD REVEALED TO MY FRIEND AND BETHANY SUNDAY, APRIL 2, 2023

My Special Friend said to me that husband and wife are you and me, so you are the only one that can make me feel like a person that I am not sure that I can be.

I said to him that, yes, you can; you are that person. God has been trying to get your attention. God chose you to minister. There are people that only you can reach. God chose us to minister together to those people. This is God's will, plan, and purpose for you husband and me wife, together. God is wanting to bring unity to the church. You husband and me wife will obey God together as one. You are a leader; I am your helper. He will give us His Words to speak at His right time. The Lord will give us direction; He will teach us; He will guide our footsteps, slowly and surely. His Word tells us not to think what we should speak; the Holy Spirit will speak through us. He will tell us what to say.

I told him that God chose us in our later years to work for Him. As we share our love for each other, we will share God's love to our families and friends, that they will be saved. I am excited about what God has plainly revealed to us about His will, plan, and purpose for us that we were chosen together for this time in our lives.

I said, Sweeheart, I did not know all of this until just now when God revealed it to us. I often wondered why. I knew it was not just for us to marry to be together for the rest of our lives; it is more; we are chosen to work together as one. You just keep talking to people as you have been doing. They thought you were a preacher, but you said that you are a man of God. You and I are messengers, like the angels in Heaven are messengers.

He said to me that he will be with me the rest of his life, helping with our Stay Focused Messages. He said that I want to give you a good idea about what you want to know about me and how I feel about you. You are the only one who has been able to help me out with this problem. I love you so very deeply, and I hope that you can help me make these things happen.

On April 9, 2023, my special friend said that when you get some time to go out to dinner with me, when you get back from your trip, I will let you know when we can meet. I will be happy for you to come to my house for the rest of the day, so we can talk and get to know each other better.

BETHANY'S OPEN VISION REVELATION

The Lord told me that it is His will for my special friend and me to be together, married, as one. Satan has fought us from the beginning. He does not want God's will to be done. He knows that it weakens his kingdom. He loses souls that he thought he had. Time is short. We must take the Kingdom of God by force. My thoughts of my open visions became clearer. I remembered my mom's dreams that she wrote in a letter about my sister and her husband. It was a personal dream that God had chosen them to be married, husband and wife. There were several times when Mom had dreams about their situation. From those dreams that Mom had, she knew that the enemy was fighting against God's will for their lives. Mom prayed and talked to God, each step. The longer that time went on, her dreams about the enemy seemed to get more intense. The devil did not want that couple to unite as one, but Mom, the Prayer Warrior, did not give up. She held on to what God spoke to her. She knew without a doubt that it was God's will, plan, and purpose for their lives. When you know, you stay in the fight because you are fighting for the Kingdom of God, eternal life for souls. This opened my understanding to what was going on in my life. I knew from the beginning, giving my will over to God, that the enemy would attack me. He knew that I laid my life on the line for God, my family, friends, and whosoever. The souls of His people, His creation is the most important work that we can do for His Kingdom. Save souls!

SUMMARY

Bethany Joyce Temple's beginning was July 17, 1950. Satan was angry with Dad and Mom, G.I. and Margaret Florene Wilson Temple. They turned from Satan when they repented of their sins and proclaimed Jesus Christ as their Lord and Savior. First, he attacked me with blindness; second, he used a tornado to destroy the end of the house where I was sleeping. I was lost until the angel of the Lord delivered me to my family in a flash of lightning. Satan was determined to destroy me. I was a chosen daughter from my beginning, to go forth in God's perfect will, plan, and purpose for my life. July 31, 2021, the day of our Temple Family Reunion, I cried out to God before witnesses, praying, asking for God's perfect will to be done in me. This started the beginning of my last transition on the earth until my death. I pray that I fulfill what God has chosen me to do. I want to hear God say, "Well done thy good and faithful servant. Enter into the joys of the Lord."

To God be all glory and praise! Amen

BETHANY JOYCE TEMPLE

ABOUT THE AUTHOR

My parents, G.I. Temple, and Margaret Florene Wilson Temple, had eight children. I am their last child. I married and divorced Lawrence Smith. We have five children.

My children are Lawrence Dion Smith, married Heather Pyle Rogers; Sidney Lynn Smith; Tony Clay Smith, married Ashley Nicole Smith Smith; Amy Yvette Smith married Louis Rios; Shanara Angelle Smith married Scott Smith.

My thirteen grandchildren are Nicholas Brandon Smith, Tony Clay Smith, Jr., Colton Garrett Smith, Sadie Marie Smith, Emily Ann "Miracle" Smith, Moses Ian Rios, Cheyenne Nilda Rios Stevens, Angel Joyce Rios, Xavier Dexter Odamus Rios, Richard Scott Smith, Noah Alexander Autin, Raven Amelia Coats, Luna Ashlyn Coats.

I was born July 17, 1950. My ministry is entitled "Stay Focus Messages" which consists of 62 contacts. I had written 21 gospel songs. Seventeen of them are copyrighted in the Library of Congress. My prayer is that everyone who reads this book will be ministered to, spiritually and naturally. The Holy Bible is like a two-edged sword.

www.ingramcontent.com/pod-product-compliance
Lightning Source LLC
Chambersburg PA
CBHW041127110526
44592CB00020B/2717